This is Gail

D0807329

This is Gail

Life with and after
Chris O'Brien

Juliette O'Brien

HarperCollins*Publishers*

HarperCollins*Publishers*

First published in Australia in 2016
This edition published in 2017
by HarperCollins*Publishers* Australia Pty Limited
ABN 36 009 913 517
harpercollins.com.au

HarperCollins*Publishers*
Level 13, 201 Elizabeth Street, Sydney, NSW 2000, Australia
Unit D1, 63 Apollo Drive, Rosedale, Auckland 0632, New Zealand
A 53, Sector 57, Noida, UP, India
1 London Bridge Street, London SE1 9GF, United Kingdom
2 Bloor Street East, 20th floor, Toronto, Ontario M4W 1A8, Canada
195 Broadway, New York, NY 10007, USA

National Library of Australia Cataloguing-in-Publication data:

O'Brien, Juliette, 1984– author.
  This is Gail: life with and after Chris O'Brien / Juliette O'Brien.
  978 1 4607 5287 6 (paperback)
  978 1 4607 0357 1 (ebook)
  O'Brien, Gail.
  O'Brien, Gail — Family.
  Life change events.
  Bereavement.
  Self-actualisation (Psychology)
  Self-realisation.
920.720994

Cover design by HarperCollins Design Studio
Cover photograph of Gail O'Brien by Steve Baccon
Typeset in Bembo Std by Harper Collins Design Studio
Printed and bound in Australia by McPherson's Printing Group
The papers used by HarperCollins in the manufacture of this book
are natural, recyclable products made from wood grown in sustainable
plantation forests. The fibre source and manufacturing processes meet
recognised international environmental standards, and carry certification.

For my brother James.
More I love you and learn from you.

CONTENTS

'Because, look, even the missing are there, the gone and taken are with them in the shade pools of the peppermints by the beautiful, the beautiful the river. And even now, one of the here is leaving.'
— *Tim Winton*, Cloudstreet

'"Don't worry, darling. I'll be all right," I reassured her, a mountaineer tumbling into a bottomless crevasse and calling back with unfounded confidence to his lifelong climbing partner.'
— *Chris O'Brien*, Never Say Die

Introduction

One night in 2013, about four years after my father died, my mother, grandmother and I were enjoying a meal of comfort food at a small table in Nana's neat kitchen. Suddenly my mother started spluttering and dry retching. To my horror, she looked to be choking. I started to stand, preparing myself to perform the Heimlich manoeuvre. But before I could help, Mum swiftly and nimbly reached her fingers down her own throat and extracted a mouthful that contained a potentially murderous chicken bone. Nana — a matter-of-fact woman in her mid-eighties who never endorses fuss — rolled her eyes and said in her gentle Irish brogue, 'For goodness sake, Gail.' Mum defended herself as having come close to death, left with no choice but to regurgitate onto the tablecloth her chicken and green beans.

We started to giggle, partly at Nana's reaction, and partly at Mum's uncharacteristically abandoned table manners. How farcical it would have been, I said, if she had actually suffered an inglorious demise as the result of choking on a chicken bone at Nana's kitchen table. Soon we had to hold our sides. My mother's body was pitching back and forth with laughter. I paused and watched her for a moment. Her luminous smile seemed to fill the room. She was laughing so completely it was as if time stood still. I had thought we might never laugh so wholeheartedly again. Yet, here she was. Surely for my mother to laugh like that, after years of such sorrow and heartache, is a symptom of something magnificent inside.

My mother cared for my father — her beloved husband — as he died. She helplessly tried to halt the progress of his brain tumour as if trying to stop an avalanche crashing down a mountain. As those treacherous cells clawed their way further into his beautiful brain, my strong robust father — himself a world-renowned cancer surgeon — became completely dependent on her. Her embrace of this role sent their love and marriage to divine heights.

Caring for him was all-consuming, exhausting and dreadful in the truest sense of the word. Losing him was even worse.

The night my father died on 4 June 2009, a thick fog covered the city. Standing by his bed with my mother behind me, I watched through the window of the hospital room as it rolled in, curling around the Sydney University spires towards us, an ominous mist coming to carry him away. After we arrived home, I walked into my parents' bedroom. I found my mother sitting on the bedroom floor weeping and broken down, newly widowed, facing a life without him.

Life went on but then it crumbled when, almost two years later, my elder brother failed to do the simplest of things: to breathe in his sleep. A brave and strong young man with a strapping physique, burly arms and big hands with knuckles like marbles, Christopher Adam O'Brien was a dutiful police officer and security guard and a gentle son, brother and partner. At the age of twenty-nine he suffered a fatal seizure while he was asleep. His death left us without the comforts of legacy, some kind of longevity or the chance to say goodbye.

Through these personal tragedies, I grew to know my mother more fully. I began to recognise the tremendous spirit inside her. Beneath her tender demeanour, youthful smile and graceful touch lay a fortitude I had never realised was there.

After twenty years focused on her family and her husband's brilliant career, my mother, Gail, re-entered the workforce and returned to physiotherapy. She accepted a position on the board of the Chris O'Brien Lifehouse, diving into the depths of politics and bureaucracy without any confidence in her ability to swim. She became an advocate in her own right for compassionate and holistic cancer care.

I could attach many grand words and glorious themes to my mother's story. I could describe it as an example of grace, resilience, transcendent dedication, renewal, or a search for the meaning of it all. But ultimately Gail's is a story of love. This is the love story of a wife, of a mother, of a family.

PART ONE

A Prologue

To my dear mother,

The other night we sat in the car trying to decide which restaurant to choose — Thai or French. I called for a swift decider with sudden-death Scissors Paper Rock. We pumped our fists ('SCI-ssors, PAY-per, ROCK') and both landed on scissors. We replayed and produced clenched fists — two rocks. Then we each went for scissors again. And after the fourth attempt, at the sight of two palms stretched out into paper, I groaned and slapped my hand on my forehead while you giggled, seemingly with delight.

Growing up, I was my father's daughter. But in recent years, I think I've grown to become more like you. I want you to know that I appreciate that more and more.

With love, Juliette

Young Gail Bamford

An obstetrician arrived at the nursing facility in Baggot Street, Dublin, on 26 July 1954, and started sprinting up the stairs before he tripped and tumbled all the way back down. On the top storey, Grace Bamford was in labour with her second child. She wasn't fazed when told the doctor couldn't tend to her because he was sprawled on the footpath with a broken leg. A practical and steely woman who had grown up in the tiny coastal Northern Ireland village of Portaferry, Grace had delivered her first child at the age of twenty-three in a makeshift maternity room in the home of a coalminer in Tweefontein, South Africa. In central Dublin and two years older, she had had nothing to worry about. Fortunately, a substitute doctor soon arrived. And moments later, so did the child — my mother. She was named 'Gail', meaning 'father's joy'.

Grace's husband, Murray, thought the story of his second child's birth was hilarious and recounted it ever afterwards. As a general practitioner he delivered countless babies himself, from Dublin's grand Rotunda Hospital to single-room homes in the city's slums and remote mud-brick huts in Zululand, South Africa.

Murray, a farm boy with an adventurous spirit, had been born in a majestic farmhouse named Lisnaroe just outside the town of Clones in county Monaghan — rural farmland in southern Ireland's far north. The Irish border dissected the farm itself, causing no end of troubles for the family, with IRA farmhands and King George's police making demands. During World War I, when Protestant Northern Ireland endured rationing and Catholic southern Ireland enjoyed abundance, simply moving cattle from one paddock to another was akin to smuggling. But young Murray, whose family was Protestant, was perfectly content among the fields, orchards and lake until the age of nine when his older brothers unforgivably suggested that he be sent to school. He excelled despite the late start and went on to study medicine at Trinity College, Dublin where, at a local dance in Dublin city, he met Grace Burrows. She was an elegant and statuesque bank clerk with pale blue-green eyes, and Murray chauffeured her home on his bicycle crossbar.

The pair married two years later on 8 September 1951, and over the next sixteen years Grace gave birth to six children in three continents. Adele was born in South Africa, where African neighbours were mesmerised by the little girl with white skin and red hair who spoke Afrikaans. Gail was born in Dublin, after which the family moved to England where Murray served as a doctor and officer in the Royal Air Force. Adrienne was born in Cheltenham, England and Murray (Jnr) at Roughton Base General Hospital in Wiltshire. Linda and Michael were born some years later after the family had immigrated to Sydney, Australia.

Some of Gail's earliest memories come from Lisnaroe, the farm where her father was born and that had been in the family for generations. She and her older sister, Adele, romped down the avenues, wandered through the fields and scrambled up haystacks. They delighted in secretly tasting ripe red tomatoes in the greenhouse and stealing peas from the neighbouring farm. They would shriek with fear at the sight of their neighbour, who would shout out, 'Oye see ya, ya little Bamford girls!' and playfully chase them away.

As a child Gail Bamford had neat blonde hair, wide brown eyes and dreamy ways. By the time she started school, getting dressed in the morning was a ritual of getting no further than lifting the dress over her head. Before she had managed to slide her arms through the sleeves she would be distracted, usually by a book filled with pictures of ballerinas. Her mother, Grace, would find Gail bent over the bed wearing just her underpants and uniform draped about her neck. 'Geel, get a move on!'

Gail experienced surreal episodes where unremarkable happenings took on a cinematic feel as actors moved through their roles: cars rolled without speed; a woman bent down slowly and deliberately to a child; a man parked a truck with graceful precision. She would watch the scene with intense awareness and feel like a member of an audience before being snapped back into reality where the world found its pace and clamour again.

'You're going to be a dunce when you grow up,' Adele told her little sister. With fiery red hair and long legs, Adele seemed smarter, could run faster and was generally better at everything, at least in her little sister's eyes. But for Gail, the word 'dunce' conjured images of tutus and dance slippers. 'That's what I want to be! I want to be a dunce,' she retorted.

In 1959 with Cold War tensions high, Murray wanted to move his family as far away from Europe as he could. Their destination was determined by the responses he received from various medical associations: no reply from America; a bizarrely insulting one from Canada that implied Irishmen did not bathe every day; and a warm and encouraging letter from the Australian Medical Association. The decision was made.

Australia was a land of sunshine and opportunity, luring people to its shores with subsidised fares. Murray's and Grace's tickets cost ten pounds and the children travelled free of charge. With four children aged eight, five, three and eighteen months, thirty-two-year-old Grace and thirty-four-year-old Murray left Europe for good.

The journey at sea was five weeks aboard the *Strathaird*. A proud ocean liner that had carried the Australian cricket team nicknamed the Invincibles to England in 1948, the now sorry-looking ship was on her final voyage. In the Indian Ocean, the *Strathaird* broke down and drifted aimlessly for three days. To escape the suffocating heat of the cabin Murray took Gail and Adele up to the deck to sleep. With her hand in her father's, Gail cast her eyes over the bodies of hundreds of other passengers who had the same idea. Shimmering in breathing and sighing lines, sleeping bodies were enveloped in a darkness that seemed eternal. It was at once comforting and foreboding to the five-year-old girl.

As well as being dreamy, Gail was incurably honest. Grace took her two eldest daughters to the ship's swimming pool, where the minimum age of entry was seven.

'If anybody asks how old you are, just say "I'm seven",' Grace instructed.

A woman approached Gail as she tentatively edged her way down the ladder into the pool. 'How old are you?' she asked.

Gail felt her mother's and Adele's eyes on her as the woman repeated, 'How old are you?'

'Five,' she whispered.

Gail knew she had let her mother and sister down. They all had to leave the pool.

The ship docked at Fremantle before proceeding around the Great Australian Bight. On the trip, huge storms lashed the *Strathaird*, which violently pitched from side to side. With so many passengers suffering seasickness the decks and halls were ghostly and silent. But Gail's strong constitution was evident even then and she spent the days exploring the ship, dragging herself by thick ropes along the tilting corridors and across the deserted decks, squinting through the white ocean spray.

The grand old *Strathaird* finally docked at Sydney's Circular Quay on 1 July 1960. The Bamford family was collected by a driver and they headed for Blackheath in the Blue Mountains, where Murray Bamford had secured a job as a general practitioner. Promised sunshine and beaches, they arrived in a drab town in the middle of a chilly winter. Their new home was a dilapidated cottage where the rain leaked through the roof and they could see the snow outside through cracks in the weatherboard walls. 'Don't unpack. We're going back,' Grace announced as the tea chests were set on the ground. But they couldn't afford to leave; it had cost twenty pounds to come to Australia but would be hundreds for them all to return.

After six months in Blackheath, Murray's desire to be beside the sea took the family to Mona Vale on Sydney's northern beaches, then south to the Sutherland Shire, first in the suburb of Gymea and finally Cronulla — 'God's own country', as the locals boast. Here they discovered the sunshine and beaches they had been promised, and Murray and Grace settled there to raise their growing family.

Until she arrived in Australia my mother believed her name was 'Geel', as her parents pronounced it, not 'Gail'. 'Why do you talk like that?' the other children at school would ask. Australia seemed an alien place and other children imitating her speech soon made her modify her pronunciation. Like her sisters and brother, Gail was well spoken, immaculately dressed and impeccably behaved. The Bamford children sat quiet as church mice on the verandahs of homes to which Grace, the doctor's wife, was invited to pay a visit. Dressed in smart little kilts with matching blue-and-white blazers, they swung their legs in silence as they politely ate the horrible homemade ice cream to which they were treated.

At Gymea public school Gail and Adele were part of a small cohort of students in classrooms tucked away in the bush. Gail loved being there. She played among the roots of the big trees, sweeping them out and inviting people in, pretending it was her own living room. She would accompany her father as he worked in the yard. 'You're closest to God in the garden,' Murray would say.

One day, back in the school's main building, Gail sat in assembly with the rest of her classmates, watching while a fellow student performed a flashy dance routine, full of splits, twirls and leaps. The minute Gail arrived home she begged her parents to let her attend dance classes, and they agreed. Beverley Chatterton held children's ballet classes in the local Presbyterian church hall. At the age of nine Gail was a late starter. But she displayed natural ability and acute physical intelligence, quickly becoming the star pupil who was awarded a scholarship every year.

Gail's parents decided to send her to Methodist Ladies College, a large private girls' school in a western suburb of

Sydney, for her secondary schooling. This entailed an interview with the headmistress, for which Gail wore a mustard-coloured suit with brown trim and brown gloves. As she and her mother walked across Burwood Park, Grace said, 'Geel, when you are asked a question, you are not to say "I don't mind," do you hear?'

The headmistress, Dr Whitley, seemed stern and important. 'What are your interests?' she asked Gail.

'I like art. And I'd like to learn French or another language.'

'Which would you prefer?'

Gail paused.

'Art or languages?' Dr Whitley demanded.

Gail gulped and whispered, 'I don't mind.'

Perhaps Gail was inclined to be compliant or eager to please, yet she already showed signs of having a strong will. Her position in the A stream at school meant, to her disappointment, that she studied languages, science and maths but not cooking, sewing and art. Determinedly, she enrolled in first-level visual arts in her senior years, the only girl in her year to do so. Throughout high school she attended ballet classes nearly every night at the Hallidays academy, which meant catching the train into central Sydney. Almost every weeknight after dark she walked alone through the park adjacent to Central station and took the hour-long train trip home, arriving after 8pm — in time to eat dinner, do her homework and go to bed.

At the age of fifteen Gail had to decide whether to become a professional dancer. Murray and Grace discouraged their daughter from following a theatrical career and spelled out the benefits of a university education. Deciding her parents were right, a year or two later Gail elected to study architecture at the University of Sydney. But thanks to a silly error when filling out the application form, she found she had been admitted to agriculture instead. Her father suggested that she'd be suited to physiotherapy, prompting visions in Gail's mind of the British comedy show *Doctor in the House* in which young physiotherapists swanned around the hydrotherapy pool. She enrolled in physiotherapy at the NSW College of Paramedical Studies based at the University of Sydney.

On her first day at university, a photographer with long hair and a cigarette sitting on his lip approached and asked whether he could take her photograph. On the back cover of the *Union Recorder*'s next issue was her photo in black and white, captioned 'Gail'. We still have it. She wore little make-up and no nail polish, but was naturally beautiful, with a beauty spot on one of her glowing cheeks, fine fair hair and a direct and candid smile. It was a photograph that would come to the attention of a medical student named Chris O'Brien.

Falling in Love

The year 1975 was drawing to a close. Gail and her best friend, Jenny, sat in a noisy pub near the university. They had both completed the three gruelling years of their physiotherapy course, involving viva voce exams, clinical placements and maintaining grades high enough to avoid year group culling. Many of Gail's placements were at Royal Prince Alfred (RPA), the large public teaching hospital in Sydney's inner west: now Jenny was suggesting that they should apply to work there. Gail was familiar with the dark old buildings of C and D blocks, built in 1882, as well as the Page Chest Pavilion. More time in that dingy place did not appeal to her. She had recently broken up with a long-term boyfriend and was looking for a change of scenery and more independence from her parents.

Gail wanted to go to Newcastle or perhaps a country hospital, as she told Jenny. 'You can go to the country later,' Jenny said. 'Just come to RPA with me for a year. We'll earn lots of money and go travelling together.' It was tempting; Jenny was smart to appeal to Gail's desire to go overseas. Still dancing every day, she yearned to attend professional ballet classes in Europe. RPA had a reputation as one of the best placements for providing enormous experience and a diverse workload. More importantly with overtime they could earn good money. And so they both applied to RPA and were accepted.

Young physiotherapy residents at RPA had enormous responsibility. On her first weekend Gail worked day and night, putting orthopaedic patients into traction, applying plasters to arms and legs in emergency, percussing chests in intensive care, suctioning and changing tracheotomy tubes as well as administering chest physiotherapy to patients throughout the main hospital. She worked two twenty-two-hour shifts and was back at work on Monday morning. There was no such thing as time off in lieu. The overtime was limited only by hours in the day.

Gail's first ward placement was the head and neck ward. Head and neck treatment involves the soft tissues of those areas, such as the mouth, throat, sinuses and salivary glands, and secondary cancers in the lymph glands of the neck. Gail changed scores of tracheotomy tubes in these patients and administered physiotherapy to poor immobile bodies. Many patients were unable to speak, chew or swallow. Some had undergone a 'commando' operation — a huge procedure involving the removal of the tongue, mandible and/or lymph nodes in the neck. An acronym for combined mandibulectomy and neck dissection operation, the 'commando' involved transporting a piece of skin from the chest to the face, forcing patients to languish in hospital for weeks while the flap of skin took to its new surrounding tissue and blood supply.

Late in January 1976, the medical residents and interns invited the new physio residents to a welcome party in their quarters. A group of girls gathered in Gail's room, strategically delaying their entrance. There was a knock on the door and in breezed an extremely attractive young doctor, with thick wavy hair, black eyebrows, green eyes and a Zapata moustache. He was wearing short white shorts and a Hawaiian shirt. 'Are you girls coming to the party or what?' he asked the room. Gail was drawn to him immediately.

Chris O'Brien was a medical resident from Sydney's western suburbs, the middle of three children. His mother, Maureen, was a dynamic, gregarious school headmistress. She read voraciously and could carry on three conversations at the same time. She had been the bedrock of the family during Chris's youth; his father, Kevin, bore mental scars from fighting in Singapore as a teenager during World War II. Chris's older brother, Michael, was a livewire and a wit; he and Chris would encourage each other in *Goon Show*–style hilarity that would have everyone in stitches. Carmel, the youngest, spent her childhood trotting after her two older brothers as they engaged in harmless mischief such as throwing stones at passing trains and making themselves sick by smoking their father's cigars.

Chris had star quality. At his high school, Parramatta Marist Brothers, he had been a charismatic, popular, rugby league–playing, premiership-winning school captain. He was a devout Catholic as an adolescent and conscientious objector with a strong sense of social justice. Although, like Gail, he had considered studying architecture, his values led him to study medicine instead.

Chris and Gail had walked the same paths and hallways of the university for the previous three years without ever meeting, but once they had met they kept coming across each other. They found themselves standing side by side in line at the canteen. They ran into each other outside Balmain's Unity Hall where a somewhat inebriated Chris tried to elicit an introduction to her. Then one day Gail walked past Chris in a hospital hallway. He made his move with a smooth line: 'Hmmm, is that Y by Yves Saint Laurent you're wearing?' Gail tilted her head and shrugged her shoulders. But inside she squealed, *yes*!

A few days later, Chris asked Gail for her telephone number. When he rang the Bamford family home, Murray called out, 'Geely! It's a Chris O'Brien on the phone for you.' And then as he handed her the phone he added, 'O'Brien. That's a very Catholic name.' She cringed and slid around the corner for privacy, pulling the telephone's cord as far as it could stretch.

Gail didn't care whether O'Brien was a Catholic surname: she liked the Irishness of it. Like everything else about Chris, it seemed just right. He was boundlessly energetic and, like her, filled his life with work, a hectic social scene and physical activity. He jogged and played rugby, tennis and golf (or at least attempted the latter). He represented Prince Alfred in inter-hospital rugby competitions, and occasionally Gail would wander over to St John's oval and watch him play. For the first few months the pair weren't dating exclusively. In fact, on one occasion Gail was waiting to say hello to Chris after a game while another of his admirers did the same. But by the end of the year they were an item.

Gail was living in the residents' quarters at RPA, but Chris shared an apartment with two friends. Their place regularly saw rowdy dinners where garden furniture was dragged inside to seat twenty or more at a long makeshift table. Their culinary expertise often left something to be desired. One evening Gail walked through the paint-flaking doorway to find Chris and a flatmate shovelling rice out the window.

'I think we put too much rice in the pot and it's overflowing like it's alive,' Chris shouted over his shoulder.

'How much did you put in?' she asked.

'Um, well, we figured it was a cup per person. So we put in twenty cups.'

Gail took the overflowing pot off the stove and tried to subdue the gluggy mess. Later, Chris took cheeky delight in the fact that their guests had seen her at the stove and mistaken the disastrous meal as her doing.

One day at the Bodenweiser Dance Centre near Broadway where she was still training, Gail spotted a pamphlet for a summer course in Paris to study fine and performing arts and French language. Her desire to go overseas was undiminished and she saw this as a perfect opportunity. She mentioned it to Chris over dinner that night and, in what she interpreted as a grand gesture of his commitment, he asked whether she would wait a few months so he could go with her. Chris had to complete two more short secondments as part of his training. The first was at Dubbo Base Hospital and he suggested Gail go there with him. She agreed and also worked there as a physio. Despite her parents' disapproval, Gail and Chris lived together in the residents' quarters.

It wasn't long before Chris was inviting hospital colleagues home for dinner parties, and the number of guests regularly ballooned to more than a dozen. It could have been seen as presumptuous for a twenty-five-year-old surgical resident to invite senior surgeons, anaesthetists and their spouses to his quarters for a dinner hosted by himself and his twenty-two-year-old girlfriend, but Chris and Gail didn't think twice. Together, they were natural entertainers. She cooked spaghetti bolognaise while he topped up glasses with cheap wine. Gail was besotted: life with Chris O'Brien was exciting and fun. And when in the hospital she saw him tenderly nursing a tiny baby just a few weeks old, she knew she wanted to marry him.

At the conclusion of Chris's Dubbo secondment, the pair travelled back to Sydney. Because Gail had planned to go overseas, she hadn't applied for a second-year residency at Prince Alfred. While Chris completed his second secondment she bided her time by working at a private orthopaedic practice in Sydney's inner west for a surgeon who drove a Rolls-Royce, wore a gold watch on one arm with usually a platinum blonde on the other and where patient numbers swelled with mysterious work-related back injuries. Gail hated working there, but continued as she waited for Chris.

Just before the pair were finally about to set off for Paris, Gail's father, Murray, gently chided, 'I don't believe that you should have the honeymoon before the wedding.' Impulsively, the young couple agreed that they should be engaged for the sake of their parents. Murray and Grace were elated, as were Chris's parents, Kevin and Maureen.

But Gail could see that Chris was perhaps not quite ready for this move. She let him off the hook by saying she didn't think the timing or reason were right. When she saw the relief on his face she knew she had guessed correctly. But her parents weren't so pleased. As an engagement present, they brought to dinner a beautiful set of cutlery. 'Mum, I'm sorry but we've decided not to get engaged just yet,' Gail said. When Grace and Murray left, Grace took the cutlery set with her.

The first stop on their premature 'honeymoon' was Ireland, where Gail took Chris to meet her family in Malahide, a beautiful coastal village forty minutes north of Dublin by car. Grace's brother Hugh and his wife, Clonagh, welcomed their niece and her boyfriend with a sherry. Then Hugh awkwardly explained that there was only one spare bedroom in the house. For the sake of Gail's elderly and conservative grandmother, they had borrowed a caravan that could accommodate Chris. It was sitting in the garden.

From Ireland they travelled to Paris, ready for a summer in continental Europe. They enrolled in a six-week course at the Paris American Academy and rented a tiny studio apartment on the Boulevard Raspail in Montparnasse. After language and history classes in the morning, Gail spent the afternoons immersed in ballet and French cuisine where a temperamental chef would shout at his students 'chaud chaud chaud' as he ran from the oven with a hot tray. Chris took classes in painting and photography. He visited Gail in the dance studios and took beautiful black-and-white photographs of her. We still have them.

Their budget was five dollars a day, which meant picnic dinners that were cheap but romantic with food and wine from a local charcuterie. They discovered Le Dôme café on the Boulevard du Montparnasse and it became one of their favourite places. Here they would enjoy a kir — white wine with a few drops of crème de cassis. For years after, my father would pour the same drink for my mother in the early evening, handing it to her as he leaned into her smile for a kiss, both transported back to those Parisian summer days.

After a couple of months in Paris, Gail and Chris bought a small second-hand Renault and set off around Europe, following the roads to Belgium, Germany, Austria, Italy and Switzerland. Gail's French and German were slightly better than Chris's, but he had more nerve, and would simply make up words he didn't know with a French or German accent. '*In Winterthur bist sie verkin?*' he asked a loud group of smoking and drinking Germans in the restaurant carriage of a train. Gail pointed out through her giggles that '*verkin*' wasn't a word and that if he was trying to say 'working' the correct word was '*arbeiten*'. But Chris spoke so confidently that the Germans responded without hesitation.

Towards the end of the trip Chris developed tonsillitis and was very unwell with fevers, chills and throat pain. Gail cared for him, feeding him and wrapping him in warm blankets. It was the most severe illness Gail would see him suffer until decades later.

When the time came for Chris to go back to Sydney to complete his surgical training as a resident medical officer, Gail decided to stay on and travel to London. She found a room at the YWCA in Chelsea and took professional-level ballet classes at Covent Garden. A fellow student asked her whether she wanted to make extra money by covering some shifts at a retail shop nearby. Gail jumped at the chance and showed up for work. The store turned out to be a sex shop that attracted a lonely and quiet clientele where Gail would sit at the counter and pass the time knitting, pointing out this product or that item to customers.

She arrived back in Sydney with a letter of recommendation from her Covent Garden instructor addressed to the Australian Ballet's Dame Peggy van Praagh. But she never followed it through. Ultimately, she didn't believe that she could become a prima ballerina, and unconsciously her life and plans had moved away from dance.

Her reunion with Chris was passionate but she was crestfallen to discover that things between them seemed unchanged. One night over dinner she asked him where their relationship was going. 'You know that I have to do a secondment in Darwin for a while,' Chris said.

Gail realised that this could mean further months of waiting. *If he's not sure of me now, after all our time together, he never will be*, she decided. 'Well, in that case I'm going to start seeing other people,' she said. Chris was spurred to action; before he left for Darwin he proposed.

Chris and Gail married on 16 February 1980, in the Great Hall of the University of Sydney. The Catholic ceremony, attended by about a hundred guests, was followed by a simple reception in the Holme Building, part of the Sydney University Union complex and very close to the Great Hall. There were no wedding cars; just the family cars driven by friends. A friend was asked to record the day on the family video camera but his obsession with planes resulted in a recording that has the camera veering towards the sky every time a passenger jet went overhead. (The friend later became a Qantas pilot.)

Gail wore a white lace crinoline-style dress she had found and bought cheaply (and optimistically) in London. She matched it with a wide-brimmed hat, lace gloves and a parasol, and was feminine beauty personified. Chris looked dashing in tails and gloves. She walked towards him on her father's arm while Offenbach's 'Barcarolle' rang out from the grand organ. As her hand was passed to that of her new husband, Gail felt a strong sense of symbolism now sometimes considered antiquated and patriarchal, telling herself: *I am no longer Gail Bamford, I am Gail O'Brien.*

To my dear mother,

To think of you on your wedding day, and all that lay ahead: you at twenty-five, Dad twenty-eight. On the edge of a life together, with no concept of how much greater than the sum of its parts your union would be.

You have a photo of Dad that he has written on. It says something about soulmates. What did you think of soulmates on your wedding day? And what do you think of them now?

With my love, Juliette

* * *

My darling Juliette,

My favourite photo of your father was taken when he was the director of the Sydney Cancer Centre in 2003. It is the photo that appeared on all the SCC documentation, newsletters and reports.

It is symbolic of an immensely happy time in our lives. He was charisma personified with his black Irish good looks and humour and I believe this photo captures his essence.

I remember handing this photo to him and saying, 'I love this photo of you, honeybunny. Will you please write on it for me?' It seems an odd request to make of your husband but we both knew what it meant: he wrote what we were unable to articulate otherwise. 'To my darling Pinkie my eternal soulmate. Thank you for sharing my life.' ('Pinkie' was his nickname for me since shortly after we started dating, inspired by my blushing at something he had said.) When he had finished writing, his handwriting now shaky but his mind clear and strong, our eyes lingered on his words and this undeniable truth. 'Thank you,' I said without looking into his eyes, 'that's beautiful.'

The force of attraction that originally brought your father and me together which we refer to as 'chemistry' is a mystery indeed. Does that immortal part of us, our souls, find each other through some celestial contract and dovetail to unity? Or does the soul need time to bond with her mate? Whatever it may be, your father and I were soulmates. We completed each other and our union was to last the test of time with all its highs and lows.

In his younger days your father's intellect and pragmatism told him that in reality there must be hundreds of partners available to any one of us. But I knew from the beginning that we were supposed to be together. It all felt right, even his name, the Irishness of it.

With the benefit of life experience, I realise that the bride and groom grew far more in their human experience through the adverse situations that they confronted head on together over the years, rather than through the comfortable and privileged lifestyle to which they had become accustomed.

Your father's resolve to survive that horrible disease as long as he could took steely determination and tenacity for us both. A life-threatening illness affects the whole family and takes its toll on the carer, physically, mentally and emotionally. I believe your father was so grateful that I did not falter under the pressure. Perhaps that was the turning point in his thinking. Perhaps without all the previous distractions prior to his illness, he could now see the truth.

Love, Mum

Embarking Together

Christopher Adam O'Brien was the most beautiful baby. Born on 16 October 1981 he had light blue eyes, blonde hair and pale eyebrows, so fair that a colleague of Chris's compared him to a milk bottle. He was named after his father but known as Adam.

His delivery had been traumatic. The labour lasted twenty-one hours and included a failed forceps delivery that damaged Gail's sciatic nerve and caused her to walk with a foot drop for weeks. Adam was finally delivered via a crash caesarean section, but was flaccid and turning blue. A young anaesthetist fumbled when intubating him, tempting Chris to grab the tube out of the young man's hands and do it himself.

But Adam was physically robust from the beginning and quickly started to breathe on his own. He was naturally bright and inquisitive. He would lean out of Gail's backpack as she carried him around, peering and smiling at people with interest. 'What a great baby!' a stranger said as Gail wandered through the Balmain markets. He grew up to be a healthy, strong little boy, athletic and coordinated, mastering things quickly, riding a bicycle without training wheels at the age of three.

Chris and Gail were living in a terrace house in the cramped inner-city suburb of Balmain. They brought their baby home and introduced him to the neighbourhood. One neighbour, Rex, had a giant basset hound that also happened to be called Adam.

'What's your baby's name?' Rex asked Chris.

'Well, actually, it's Adam.'

'Adam? But that's a dog's name.'

'No, Rex is a dog's name, Rex.'

Money was tight. Chris had sacrificed his resident's salary to complete a master's degree in surgery. He was studying microvascular surgery — a surgical technique that involves operating on tiny blood vessels perhaps only three millimetres in diameter. He and Gail were living on a research grant and needed to find a more affordable home. Chris happened to be turning into Westbourne Street, Drummoyne, at the moment when a real estate agent was putting up a sign in front of a semi-detached house: 'For Sale: Deceased Estate'. Chris asked to see inside.

'Are you ready for a shock?' asked the agent as he swung open the door.

It was a derelict house with an outdoor toilet and crumbling kitchen. But it had high ceilings, a view of Five Dock Bay and it was larger than any of the apartments they had seen. Chris and Gail quickly made an offer and moved in before anyone else knew the house was even on the market.

'We seem to have luck on our side,' said Gail.

'Three togethers forevers,' Chris said as the small family made the house their own.

Two years later on 1 February 1984, I was born and 'four togethers' didn't have quite the same ring. Asthmatic, I didn't have my brother's robustness and I certainly lacked his coordination (requiring training wheels on my bike until I was seven) plus I had the bandiest little legs anyone who knew me had ever seen. But I was placid and generally healthy, and my dark hair and olive skin formed an apparently pleasing ebony contrast to my ivory brother.

After my mother had given birth to me, she saw her obstetrician. 'How are you?' Dr Bob Lyneham asked.

She felt sore and frumpy. 'I'm not the woman I was,' she told him.

'Better,' he replied.

A few months later Gail pushed her double pram up the hill towards a supermarket, while cars roared by and the forty-degree Sydney summer heat radiated from the pavement. An elderly lady passing by smiled at my brother and me, looked up at Gail and said, 'These are the best days of your life.' *God help me*, Gail thought. Her world had shrunk considerably since her second child was born. Feed. Walk. Feed. Sleep. Feed. 'I just feel like a mothering machine,' she confessed to her mother-in-law.

For the time being Gail was a stay-at-home mother. She had returned to part-time work briefly when expecting me and had not enjoyed dragging heavy medical machines into nursing homes when heavily pregnant and coming home to a baby and husband to feed. A return to work with two young children would have required some serious logistical planning. But she didn't miss physiotherapy. She wanted to be a mother, the primary carer of her children.

My father's work and surgical training were becoming more focused. He told Gail he planned to specialise in head and neck surgery, which made her recall those poor 'commando' patients whose tracheotomies she had changed as a young physiotherapist. But Chris's research had put him on the leading edge of a revolution in surgery that would see a dramatic improvement in quality of life for head and neck patients. Newly developed reconstructive surgical techniques meant that major operations on the mouth, tongue, mandible and neck, formerly so disfiguring, could have radically improved outcomes. Chris's training required stints overseas to work in multidisciplinary teams. He successfully applied for placements at London's Royal Marsden Hospital and the comprehensive cancer clinic at the University of Alabama in Birmingham (UAB). Chris and Gail packed up my two-year-old brother and five-month-old me, and we flew to England.

In Chelsea, London, our apartment was in a dilapidated building with dark hallways that smelled of curry. The flat was just one room with a shower in the corner. As Chris had signed for the keys, the landlady had looked at Gail, Adam and me and said, 'I don't think your wife is going to like it here.' The landlady was right, but the prospect of finding anything better on their limited money from the university grant was remote. However, within days Chris and Gail discovered that postgraduate accommodation had just become available in the north London suburb of East Finchley. This was a flat with a separate kitchen and bedroom and a small garden. Most importantly, it had friendly neighbours who were like our family — young doctors, new mothers and small children. 'The lucky O'Briens strike again,' Chris said. It would become an oft-repeated line.

After a year we moved to Birmingham, Alabama, in the USA's Deep South. The city felt like a moonscape with wide, flat, hot roads, giant cars and tornado warnings. Gail missed the network of young families that had surrounded us in London. Chris would leave for work in the morning and without a phone or a car she had no way of contacting him. She was stuck at home with a two- and four-year-old with nothing much to do except occasionally go to the mall. But once again she showed her adaptability, making friends with Japanese, Chinese, English and African-American neighbours, joining a club of 'international mothers' and volunteering to teach dance classes to children with disabilities.

Over the next two years Chris and Gail built up lives and social circles, but no sooner had Adam and I perfected our southern twangs than we were packed up and moved again.

This time we returned to Sydney and Chris went back to RPA. He was appointed visiting medical officer (VMO) in head and neck surgery, an important milestone that meant he had his own consulting rooms. The rooms became almost an O'Brien family business, with Gail managing the practice, overseeing staff, finances and logistics and working as secretary when necessary. The decision that Chris and Gail would run the practice together completely entwined her life and work with that of her husband.

As she worked in the rooms, Gail was acutely aware of the tragic pathologies of some of Chris's patients. A young female patient arrived one day and Gail saw on her file she was to undergo a 'commando'. It was the first such patient she'd come across for years. Her heart went out to the woman, who she envisaged would be stuck in the hospital for weeks as the flap of skin took. But a couple of weeks later, the same woman returned. After her surgery she looked terrific, with a patch of skin — probably taken from her forearm — sewn neatly and subtly along her jawline.

In that moment Gail fully understood why she and their two small children had been leading an almost nomadic life and surviving on medical research grants. She knew, of course, that Chris had been working with surgical teams and studying microvascular surgery techniques, but until then she hadn't been able to put a human face or experience to this abstract quest. Now here was this young woman, recovering from this major operation in a way that would have been unimaginable a few years earlier. The new flap of skin was already nearly healed with a healthy flow of blood to the new tissue, thanks to Chris's ability to sew the tissue's blood vessels to those surrounding it. She could not have felt more proud of her husband.

Early in 1989 Gail was twelve weeks pregnant with her third child. She had just seen her obstetrician (everything seemed fine) and was hurrying down Market Street in central Sydney to catch a bus. She felt something running down her legs and looked down. It was blood. A scan revealed placenta praevia, a serious condition where the placenta completely covers the cervix. She was admitted to hospital immediately and advised that she would need to stay for a number of weeks. 'I can't possibly,' she said. We had moved to a larger house a few streets away in Drummoyne and the renovations were ongoing. Adam and I were both at the local public school, with a busy schedule of after-school activities of sports, dance and music classes. Chris was working long days and weeks and Gail was still managing the ever-expanding business.

After a few days, she was allowed home under strict instructions to stay in bed. She would prop up her head as much as she could while still remaining horizontal, helping Adam with his homework, supervising my scratching on the violin, doing the practice's finances and arranging house renovations. But after waking in the night to find the sheets and mattress soaked with blood, she was finally transported to King George V women's hospital via ambulance. She stayed in hospital for the next ten weeks.

My father found this period immensely difficult, requiring military-standard coordination to manage all the needs of two young children plus dealing with long operating lists and consulting days. Family helped — Gail's mother, Grace, would stay with us for a couple of days at a time to be replaced by Chris's mother, Maureen. A nanny supervised some afternoons and cooked dinners that I considered foreign and strange. The carrots were cut the wrong way and the lamb chops had a peculiar flavour. Adam, buoyant as always, was indifferent to such details, but I was — and still am — uncomfortable with change. We were both oblivious to any strain on our dad. He'd arranged his days to start work a little later, and I loved having him brush my hair in the morning. He would pull it back into a ponytail gently and tenderly, in stark contrast to my grandmothers' tugging.

From her hospital bed in King George V, Gail continued doing administrative work for the practice and even took the time to become an Australian citizen. The other women in her room revealed a range of pregnancy complications: Martha had gestational diabetes and would suffer diabetic fits; Sue was expecting triplets; Therese went into labour six weeks early and, despite being pumped with steroids to stop the birth, had a premature baby.

On 25 October 1989 Gail was collected from the prenatal ward at seven in the morning, ready for her scheduled caesarean section. She felt confident that nothing would go wrong with this delivery, and she was right: a few hours later she was on the postnatal ward with a baby boy. He was named James Michael.

Sore and uncomfortable, Gail was trying to breast-feed James without being able to sit up properly. James pulled away from the breast and coughed in a soft whimper several times. Then his lips started to turn blue. Gail called out to a nurse and James was taken to the neonatal intensive care nursery for observation. At five o'clock the next morning a nurse came to tell Gail that her baby's condition had worsened.

Gail, in a wheelchair, looked at her baby in the humidicrib and ached at the sight of his tiny body surrounded by medical machinery. He was artificially ventilated with air being forced into his lungs at high pressure and multiple tubes leading in and out of him as drugs tried to dilate the vessels of his tiny lungs. The diagnosis was pulmonary hypertension, meaning his respiratory and circulatory systems had not adapted to breathing outside the womb. A lung collapsed and James's oxygen levels refused to stabilise. Each day brought more dire news. He wasn't expected to survive. Over the next few days his little body became so swollen with fluid that he looked twice the size of his birth weight and positively huge compared to the premature babies in the nursery. Gail struggled to grasp the reality, believing that surely at any moment someone was going to say there had been a mistake and James would survive. She stroked his little head, spoke his name and tried to get to know him. A tube was inserted into James's scalp when there were no more available veins elsewhere on his body. A young nurse named Serena (by name and by nature) clipped some of his hair for Gail to keep. Gail was handed the little memento, thoughtfully wrapped in plastic, which it seemed would be a reminder that once she did have this little boy, for a short time.

Gail had been moved to a single room, considered better for women who had given birth but didn't have the child. She felt isolated and alone. She sat on the edge of the bed, feeling so depressed she was unable to even lift a brush to tidy her hair. On top of all this she was enduring the usual post-natal night sweats and breast engorgement.

Needing help with the breast pump, Gail pressed the buzzer to summon a nurse. There was no answer and she pressed again. Eventually a harassed-looking older woman in a nurse's uniform pushed the door open and sharply asked what was wrong. Gail politely made her request and started to explain that her baby was in the nursery.

'We're very busy, Mrs O'Brien,' said the nurse. 'There are other babies in the nursery too.' Then she left. Gail felt like a naughty schoolgirl. Stunned, alone, hormonal, in pain and exhausted, she had no idea whether the nurse would bring the pump or not. She phoned Chris, wanting a few words of love and comfort. But as soon as she heard his voice she became distraught, sobbing as she recounted what had happened. Chris reassured her gently, not showing that he was enraged. He left my brother and me with a friend and drove straight to the hospital, making phone calls to the nursing hierarchy at King George V. When Chris was angry, he could be fearsome. He demanded that the nurse be sacked, and was senior enough to elicit an immediate reaction. The superintendent of nursing, looking official in her white coat, went straight to Gail's room. With Chris now standing by Gail, the superintendent apologised, although it seemed motivated more by a pragmatic calculation than genuine remorse. 'You do realise you are day three, and therefore prone to the third-day blues?' she said.

'Yes, I know all about the day-three blues,' said Gail. 'This is my third child and I've worked on the pre- and post-natal wards here.'

The woman tried another approach. 'Do you really want this nurse to be dismissed?' she asked. Chris was adamant and prepared to insist but Gail said no, she genuinely did not want that. Later, as Chris and Gail walked towards the nursery, arm in arm down the main aisle of the ward, they passed the nurse. She looked at them with an apologetic and meek expression. Gail offered her a sympathetic smile, but Chris firmly stared ahead.

My father deplored bullies and was intolerant of anyone who he considered was preying on frailty in others. In these circumstances he was just the type of person you'd want on your side: gentle and loyal to his people, but fiercely tough on intimidators. My mother is more inclined to see the best in people and quicker to forgive.

That evening, with the baby making no improvement, Chris said to Gail, 'I'd like to get a priest for James.' On the fourth day after James's birth the hospital chaplain Father James Collins blessed him and administered last rites.

After the ceremony, Chris and his sister, Carmel, walked up Missenden Road to a church to attend mass. Gail was concerned about her husband. He was pushing through the pain of their son's condition to continue working, consulting with patients and doing major operations into the night. As Chris walked inside the dim building and looked towards the altar, he saw a long white banner hanging from the ceiling. Large golden letters running down it spelled out the words, 'He Lives'.

When he returned to the hospital, Gail was still sitting beside the humidicrib. Her eyes were shining as she said, 'It seems like he might have turned a corner, Christie.' Although Chris and Gail had been advised to prepare for James's death, Professor David Henderson-Smart had not given up, administering an experimental drug called prostacyclin. For the first time, James's oxygen levels had stabilised as the drug took effect, distending his blood vessels and finally reducing the blood pressure in his lungs. His survival simply seemed a miracle. *He Lives*. Chris and Gail brought James home six weeks later. Our family of five was complete.

Riding High

I must have been about nine when I arrived home from school one afternoon to find my mother at the kitchen bench with the tail of a huge, dead fish in one hand and a large knife in the other. The beast probably weighed ten kilos and Mum was ripping the knife down its long carcass, causing shiny little scales to go popping off in every direction. 'Wow, what's that for?' I asked. I noticed her face was red.

'A patient gave your father this fish and he's invited twelve people over tonight to eat it,' she snapped. 'It's still frozen ... and *unscaled*.' She scraped the knife down again and a few more tiny, translucent pieces flew through the air. Exhaling loudly, she spat, 'How am I meant to cook this ... this ... *fucking fish*?'

My jaw dropped. I'd never heard her say that word before.

I adored my father and am certainly not the person to provide an objective view of him. But I now understand that, as my mother has said, it actually took great stamina, patience and a certain cunning to be married to Dr Chris O'Brien.

He was on full throttle most of the time from early morning rounds to late-night operating sessions and packed weekends. His production of academic papers was prolific and he squeezed exercise into his schedule, if necessary, by jogging in the extreme heat of a Saturday afternoon.

My parents' social calendar was exhausting: I have many childhood memories of Mum's perfume and Dad's cologne, the softness of their freshly powdered or shaven cheeks as they kissed me goodbye and swept out the door on the way to some function or other. The dining room was often filled with laughter and lively conversation as Dad hosted and Mum served extravagant multiple-course dinners. Dad invited people home every other week, displaying generous hospitality whether they were friends, 'orphan' trainees from overseas, or junior or senior colleagues.

None of this ever got in the way of their duties as parents. Dad rarely missed school events or Saturday sports. He coached rugby teams, was the master of ceremonies for school functions and even let Mum coax him into dancing as one of the Village People in a parents and friends' revue she choreographed at my school.

He'd often be home by 7.30pm so we could eat as a family. He received countless offers to speak at international conferences but did not travel more than three times each year to avoid spending too much time away. Mum would usually accompany him on these trips but occasionally Adam, James or I would be lucky enough to go. When it was my turn and we went to Boston I stayed in the giant hotel bed in the mornings, ordering room service and watching movies while he delivered his lectures, then in the afternoons we explored the city together, walking through Harvard University, browsing bookstores and taking photos of rows of tulips.

Since Westbourne Street, Drummoyne, we moved house no less than six times — three times in the same suburb before moving across the Gladesville Bridge to Hunters Hill. Thanks to some opportunistic purchases of rundown houses, Chris and Gail had accidentally become home renovators before it was fashionable.

Dad could be cheeky and irreverent, which sometimes prompted an attempted scolding from my mother. But she could hardly keep a straight face and Adam, James and I knew that she was as entertained as we were. Once, at a suburban restaurant where Dad's guitar teacher Peter Pik regularly performed, Pete, who specialises in finger-picking guitar, was playing beautifully and setting the mood. Dad called out, 'Why don't you sing, you bastard?' (an inside joke referring to a disastrous gig that Pete once played which he wanted to forget). 'Christie!' Mum hissed. During a family holiday to Tasmania and a visit to Port Arthur, Dad was impatient for Mum to emerge from a building in the former penal colony so we could all leave. He picked up a handful of pebbles and sprayed them over the corrugated iron roof, cupped his hands into a megaphone and trumpeted, 'Gail O'Brien, come out with your hands up.' She appeared a few minutes later with a thunderous expression.

As my brothers and I grew, so too did Dad's reputation and practice. He had become known throughout the region as a leading surgeon and cancer specialist. Mum, still operating as practice manager, regularly worked in the rooms to lend support to the secretaries.

In the late 1990s a Channel 9 television crew started work on a new reality television series, *RPA*, featuring staff and patients of Royal Prince Alfred Hospital. We all got a buzz out of seeing Dad on TV occasionally but he was soon being featured on the show so regularly that colleagues jibed it should be called 'The Chris O'Brien Show'. So well known did he become that in 2000 the program's producers asked him to accept a Logie award for most popular reality program. Dressing for the red carpet, Gail asked Chris's advice. 'Which colour blouse goes better with this jacket?' When she arrived at the awards night, she found herself next to a woman who was wearing the same jacket, only with no blouse at all and just one button done up at the navel.

People in the street started recognising Dad from TV; they would approach him and shake his hand. At the hairdresser one day Gail spotted a picture of him in a women's magazine above the caption 'Dr Gorgeous'. Apparently my dad was 'Dr Gorgeous' to many women. 'That's your dad?' a school peer exclaimed to me. 'Oh my God, my mum and I love him. He's so nice.' Then after a pause she added, 'His arms are a bit hairy, though.' He was public property all right. But far from being an intrusion, my brothers and I found all this quite natural. I grew up thinking that it was normal for one's father to be a surgeon everyone seemed to know.

Although I didn't understand the source of my dad's mass appeal at first, it became clearer to me over the years. His tender and humane treatment of patients seemed to be what people commented on most. They loved his bedside manner and the way he talked to people. Chris advised his trainees, 'Treat every patient as you would treat a member of your own family,' and this attitude was obvious in every episode of *RPA*. He sat on patients' bedsides and reached across tables to hold their hands. He consoled a teary wife, saying, 'Don't go out and buy black clothes,' and joked that a colleague should not say 'oops' in front of the cameras because it made him look bad. I heard stories of how he treated people when the camera wasn't there. One gentleman, a public patient, became emotional as he asked how much Chris's surgical expertise would cost. 'There's more to life than money,' Chris said as he put his arm around the man to console him. Chris's newfound minor celebrity made the practice even busier. One patient arrived with a wry referral from a GP who said that particular patient had seen Chris on television and wanted to be treated by him. 'So I have searched him all over and found a small lump on his head. Would you please remove it.'

The TV show was a bit of fun and provided some light relief, but Gail had a sense that Chris's celebrity was more significant than he knew. She observed in the practice, as it pulsed with patients, that many people there felt as if they knew her husband like he was their brother or son. But of course, much more than being a TV star, Chris was a surgeon whose focus was on contributing to improve the outcomes of cancer patients as well as building Australia's reputation for treatment and research in head and neck cancers.

In 2002 Chris told Gail about his plans to create an organisational entity to concentrate more fully on head and neck cancers. It would be called the Sydney Head and Neck Cancer Institute (SHNCI). Since working as a trainee surgeon at the University of Alabama, Chris had become an advocate for comprehensive cancer centres as the best hospital model to foster innovation, produce ground-breaking discoveries and deliver world's best practice in cancer treatment. Dozens of these types of centres existed in the United States, but no facility in Australia could meet all of the criteria. The comprehensive cancer centre model is characterised by offering patients the complete range of treatment from surgery to chemotherapy to radiation therapy, within a scientific environment that produces research, new therapies and gives patients opportunities to participate in clinical trials. The 'bench to bedside' idea of comprehensive cancer care means there is a rapid translation of research findings to improved care.

The SHNCI would be the first incarnation of Chris's dream to create a team that adopted a comprehensive approach to cancer research and care. It would bring together surgeons, radiation and medical oncologists, dental specialists, speech therapists, specialist nurses and dieticians, research scientists and data managers in a multidisciplinary setting. The institute would fund a research program that maintained a database and introduced trials to patients, and international experts would come to Sydney to undertake research and teach.

Chris had a way of tapping people on the shoulder and pulling them into his causes. At the institute's inaugural meeting almost every person on the committee had survived head and neck cancer. The faces sitting around the table at Doyles on the Beach restaurant in Watsons Bay bore evidence of Chris's surgical skill — faded scars indicating incisions, flaps or skin grafts. The Sydney seafood magnate Peter Doyle himself was there, along with a dozen or so other former patients. Every one of those people would become powerful supporters of Chris's advocacy for improving cancer care. Today, nearly fifteen years later, the loyalty of a number of them endures. Bill Conley, a partner at a major law firm, and Bob McMillan, a businessman in the printing industry, went on to become founding directors of the Chris O'Brien Lifehouse. Nat Zanardo, who until recently owned Canterbury BMW, persists in fundraising for SHNCI.

Gail's role as manager of Chris's practice expanded to the SHNCI's administration and financials. The important first task for the committee was to raise funds, and Gail stepped in to lead this. A black-tie launch for the institute was planned at Sydney's Regent Hotel (later renamed the Four Seasons). Without any real experience in fundraising, Gail set her mind to securing some big auction items. She wanted a string of pearls, relevant to head and neck surgery because it could hide a thyroidectomy scar, the most common operation that Chris did. She contacted two big pearl dealers but nobody returned her calls, despite her persistence.

By chance Gail was introduced to Bronwyn Carabez who was not a large dealer but had her own small jewellery store specialising in pearls. Bronwyn said she would love to help and arranged for the auction item and anything else the event needed, cementing Gail's faith that great generosity could be found.

As the night of the gala ball approached, Gail felt increasingly nervous. Six hundred people were coming, including the NSW health minister Craig Knowles, lord mayor of Sydney Frank Sartor, the governor of NSW Professor Marie Bashir and her husband, Sir Nicholas Shehadie. Channel 9 journalist and TV presenter Helen Dalley had agreed to be master of ceremonies.

The hotel gave Chris and Gail a room to get ready and on the night, they stood side by side at the bathroom mirror before greeting their guests. They looked at each other with a mixture of relief and disbelief. 'We did it!' Chris said. A girl from Cronulla and a boy from Regents Park were making their own reality, and their partnership was bearing fruit beyond anything they had ever imagined. The event was a great success in every way and raised over $100,000. Since then, the SHNCI has supported dozens of international fellows, from backgrounds ranging from ENT (Ear, Nose and Throat) to general plastic and maxillofacial surgery, to participate in periods of training in head and neck oncology. The institute has also contributed to research that discovered a causative link between the human papillomavirus and some head and neck cancers, especially tonsil cancer.

As well as director of the SHNCI, Chris was director of cancer services for the Sydney South West Area Health Service and clinical professor of surgery at the University of Sydney. He had founded the Australian and New Zealand Head and Neck Society, of which he became president in 2004. He trained young surgeons and teams. He lectured widely overseas, and continued writing book chapters and scientific papers, totalling more than a hundred. His private practice, by then established for more than fifteen years, was becoming overburdened as people travelled from around the city, country and Asia–Pacific region for his care. Patients were double- and triple-booked as colleagues bypassed secretaries. Chris would not say no to someone who needed to see him, and always made room for urgent cases.

When Gail provided support in the practice, the packed waiting room made her feel claustrophobic. Secretaries cowered behind their computers as throngs of patients grumbled about waiting times and expired parking meters. Chris had a way of defusing any discontent, dutifully tending to each individual and giving him or her his undivided attention. If he was late into the rooms from rounds or a meeting, he would stride in, calling, 'Don't worry, folks, doctor's here!' and elicit a smile from even the crankiest patient. On the busiest days Gail would feel so overwhelmed that she felt like she couldn't breathe. When she would leave for home in the afternoon, relieved to push through the door, she would think of Chris there in the eye of it all, slowly trudging his way through each task and patient.

Then came a new opportunity — the role of director of the Sydney Cancer Centre. It was an administrative role that would see him leading Royal Prince Alfred Hospital's cancer treatment services and it would allow him to expand his vision of research-based cancer care in the context of multidisciplinary teams. Led by a fundraising body established by Frank Sartor and chaired by Lucy Turnbull, a prominent businesswoman who succeeded Sartor as Sydney's lord mayor, the centre was planning a 'Raise the Roof' appeal to expand their premises. But the aspirations for the centre quickly grew to an entirely new building. A purpose-built centre would be the Sydney Cancer Centre's opportunity to create something that was truly comprehensive, akin to the centres of excellence in the United States.

Chris and Gail invited the New South Wales premier Morris Iemma and his wife, Santina, to dinner. Gail was happy to see that the ravenous premier wolfed down the meal she had cooked.

After dinner Chris pushed his plan, resulting in a grant of one million dollars to establish the business model. Chris was intent on trying a new model of cancer care in a privately run not-for-profit institution that was egalitarian in its admission of patients yet not controlled by the New South Wales health bureaucracy.

Gail and Chris had discussed the opportunity of Sydney Cancer Centre director as a two-days-a-week role, moving him away from work as a consulting surgeon. In fact, the result was that he had two full-time jobs. Furthermore, their fundraising efforts had grown from the SHNCI to the wider needs of the Sydney Cancer Centre. One late weeknight evening, as Chris and Gail sat in the study together auditing financials and reviewing plans for another function, Gail felt as if her rib cage was squeezing closed. 'I've got a pain in my chest,' she said to Chris.

'I used to get that. But you work through it,' he replied.

It was not the answer she wanted. Gail thought the practice was spinning out of control and that as manager she must be doing something wrong. But an expensive consultant gave her a business appraisal and offered no practical solutions, only perhaps to find more hours in the day.

Chris's load was monumental. 'Christie, we have to take some things off the list,' Gail would say. They would sit down together and list every commitment but they couldn't seem to find anything that could be crossed off. Nothing could come off the list, they said again and again. Then the decision was taken out of their hands.

Dear Mum,

I asked your close friend Di Ross for her recollections of you and our family throughout these years. After all, our families have been close since you and Di met when Adam and her oldest son, Fergus, started kindergarten together. Her response? 'Interminable violin lessons.' The patience you had to sit by Adam and me as we scratched our ways through the Busy Busy Stop Stops of 'Twinkle Twinkle Little Star'. I continued playing for fifteen years, Ad moved from violin to trombone and then trumpet. James started piano lessons — interminable is the right word!

Mum, it's clear that throughout these years your life had become completely entwined with Dad's. When I asked you about your decision to leave work and support his practice, you could not recall any conversation about it, as though your common desires to build a life together and raise a family gave rise to a mutual and effectively unspoken understanding of how that would work. I am eternally grateful for the home life that this created. But I suppose, three decades later, it would place you in a somewhat precarious position. We were completely reliant on Dad and his ability to work for security.

I wonder, what advice would you give to your younger self?

With a heart full of love and gratitude, Juliette

* * *

My dear Juliette,

The baby grand piano that sits in our living room at home bears the scars of many years of angst and resistance to practising — adds to the patina. If you look closely, you will actually find James's teeth marks on the lid from when, at the age of eight, he dropped his head out of frustration and landed his teeth in the wood! I was fascinated to learn that the Suzuki Method (which you children followed for violin and piano) places the mother in a central role for the child's learning. She must attend the child's lessons and supervise practice — she almost learns the instrument herself. That's certainly how it worked for me.

This of course assumes that the mother has the time to play this role. I did have this time, because I had stopped working as a physiotherapist. I wanted to stay at home and look after my children. I loved being a mother.

Ultimately this was my choice but sometimes our choices place us in insecure positions later on. With what was to come, I was thankful that I had never relinquished my professional registration as a physio and always kept up with continuing education. I have no regrets, Juliette. But my advice to my younger self now would be to keep her hand in what she was trained to do. Don't give it all up thinking she'll never need it again, no matter how strong the marriage is. She needs to empower herself by knowing she could cope independently if the need should arise.

Lots of love, Mum

PART TWO

In Sickness and in Health

Countdown

One evening in late November 2006, as Chris and Gail lay in bed, their bodies yielding to the exhaustion of the day, the week, the year, Gail looked at Chris's silhouette in the darkness. She knew that things were not quite right with her husband.

Outside their window, the beautiful Lane Cove River drifted gently by our Hunters Hill home. On this night, Adam, now twenty-five years old, was not at home, but his bedroom was filled with his possessions ready for his return: a weight-lifting set and bench, a 'door gym', posters of wrestlers and photos of family on the walls. He was living in Goulburn, completing his final months of training at the NSW Police Force Academy and would drive back to Sydney every few weekends and holidays. James had just turned seventeen and was now boarding at St Ignatius' College, Riverview, and preparing to enter his HSC year, in which drama and music would be his focus. I was twenty-two and had almost finished a communications degree. I was grateful to Mum and Dad for letting my boyfriend, Gareth, live with us. I felt a deep contentment when my brothers were home as well, as though the house sighed with fullness and love when we were all under the one roof.

People would come and go in a whirlwind of activity; at the time, we also had close friends from Lausanne, Switzerland, staying with us: Luc Bron and his wife, Michèle, and their baby daughter, Hélène. Luc had worked with Dad during his Ear, Nose and Throat (ENT) residency and later as a clinical fellow. He was like a member of the family.

Lying there in the darkness next to Chris, Gail remembered watching him as he strode into his consultation rooms two months before. With his thick black hair swept back and blue shirt rolled up at the sleeves, her heart had fluttered. But now his skin looked grey. She felt an intense presentiment for his responsibilities and the demands on him.

The next morning — a Thursday — Chris woke to the sound of his alarm clock with the ABC news fanfare. He dragged himself to the bathroom, stood at the basin and placed his palm over his right eye. Gail slipped out of bed and silently leaned against the doorframe. 'I've got this bad headache behind my right eye,' he muttered to no one in particular. He picked up the packet of Panadol he had used the previous few days, swallowed two pills and got ready for work.

Chris and Gail had plans to meet Luc, Michèle and other friends for dinner at a restaurant. That evening, Gail sat at the table on a Paddington footpath, waiting for Chris. The surrounding chatter faded as the minutes passed and she grew more anxious. Then, to her relief, she saw him drive past. But he passed the restaurant again and again, failing to find a parking space on the busy surrounding streets. Half an hour later, he finally appeared on foot, looking ashen. His face seemed slightly puffy and his right eye appeared to droop. 'I ran into the kerb a few times,' he murmured to her after saying his hellos. 'I just ran off to the left. It was strange.' To most at the table, he appeared somewhat rundown but still his usual self. Then he leaned over to Gail and said. 'I'm going to be sick.' They excused themselves and walked slowly down the street. Chris gulped deep breaths of air, preparing himself to vomit into a gutter, but nothing came up.

On the Friday, Chris emerged from his office and asked his assistant for more Panadol. Gail had arrived and the two women glanced at each other as Jenny popped the pills from their casing. They were at the Sydney Cancer Centre, so fortunately there were no patients for Chris to see. But a constant stream of colleagues and staff came to his office needing attention. 'Next!' he would call at the end of each meeting.

In a spare moment, Gail went to the door. Chris stood before his desk, which was piled with a chaotic mountain of paperwork. 'Look. Look at this,' he said, then held up his hands and let them fall. He looked beaten, defeated. Gail had never seen him look like this before.

On the Saturday, Gail woke early and turned off Chris's alarm clock, something she would never normally do: *I'm just going to let him sleep*, she thought. She was still thinking he had a migraine or a virus, that he was exhausted and overworked. Perhaps he still hadn't recovered from jet lag after a recent conference in the USA. She went out to do some shopping and when she arrived home he had left for his Saturday rounds and meetings.

She rang his mobile.

'Hello?' he answered in a low, soft voice.

'Oh, I'm sorry. Are you in a meeting?'

'No, I'm just so sick.'

'What's the matter with you?'

'I don't know.'

Fear swelled inside her. 'I think you should come home,' she said. At midday he arrived home and went to bed, telling her he had been forced to cut a meeting short and stop the car on the way home to be sick.

'I'm going to call tomorrow off,' Gail said, referring to a lunch they had organised at our house. But she realised she didn't have the phone numbers of the neighbours Chris had invited. She ran up the road and knocked on the door of Joe and Mel Hockey's house, explaining that they would have to cancel the lunch. She visited other neighbours with the same message: no cause for alarm, but Chris was not well.

At four o'clock, Gail rang her father for medical advice, as she had often done when the children were small. Still working as a general practitioner, nearing his sixth decade as a doctor, Murray had an encyclopaedic knowledge of medicine and Gail valued his advice over anyone's. 'Take him to the hospital,' Murray said after Gail recounted the symptoms. 'I know what you're thinking. You're thinking he has a brain tumour. Don't leave it too late. You'll never forgive yourself if you do.'

A brain tumour had not occurred to Gail. She hung up the phone as James came downstairs. It was his year eleven semi-formal and he was all dressed up in a sharp suit and with dyed blonde hair. He had just gone to show his dad how he looked. 'Jeez, Dad's not very well, Mum,' he said. 'I heard him vomiting.' Gail ran up the stairs three at a time and found Chris in the bathroom hanging over the toilet.

Bang bang! The doorknocker slammed downstairs. James opened it and welcomed a horde of excited teenagers. Gail was supposed to drive them to the pre-formal drinks.

'I'm taking you to hospital,' she said to Chris.

'Call RPA, would you?' he murmured. She knew the RPA switch number off by heart and asked to be connected with emergency, then handed the phone to Chris. He spoke to the emergency physician. 'I think I might have meningitis.'

Gail ran downstairs and greeted the beaming boys and glowing girls. Quickly she started phoning other parents, asking them to take the kids to their celebration.

Chris, standing near the car, seemed to be panicking. 'Gail, come on. Come on,' he said urgently. He sounded desperate, but Gail had no choice but to sort out the house full of teenagers. Finally the phone calls were made and she could drive Chris to the hospital.

Chris held his head in his hands on the way to the hospital and dragged himself into emergency. The triage sister greeted him, 'Oh Chris, you must be overtired or something.' He sat in a chair and Gail sat next to him, rubbing his back. Around them in the emergency waiting room, drunks argued with each other and vagrants wandered in and out. A young man with a dislocated shoulder was called, followed by an elderly woman with a wheezing chest. Chris and Gail sat there for forty minutes, waiting their turn in the hospital where Chris had worked for thirty years. The staff were busy and overworked and saw him as soon as they could. That wait marked a turning point in Chris's and Gail's lives. Life would never be the same again.

While Chris underwent a CT scan, Gail waited in a small cubicle walled in by dividers that didn't reach the ceiling. She could hear the beeps of machines attached to other people.

Eventually Chris was wheeled back with the emergency physician not far behind him. 'Chris, there is something there,' she said.

'Is it a neoplasm?' He meant a tumour.

'Yes.' She paused, then added, 'I wish I didn't have to tell you this.'

'Can it be treated?' asked Gail.

The neurosurgery registrar answered, 'Yes, it can be treated, but it's incurable.'

'Don't worry, darling. I'll be all right.' Chris reached out for Gail's hand.

Gail didn't understand. Nothing made sense. Why was everyone so quiet? Did she understand this correctly? She was already fearful. The world had tilted off its axis.

Gail called my brothers and me on our mobile phones. When she called me to say that Dad had a brain tumour, the words were barely out of her mouth when I began to sob. 'No, no, no!' I cried. With an effort, Gail kept her voice steady, repeating the simple truth. Already in the car, having just finished consecutive shifts at each of my part-time jobs, I arrived at the hospital ten minutes later. Next she called Adam in Goulburn who, with his gentle and steady nature, absorbed her words quietly, asked a few questions about Dad's physical state and resolved to drive home the following day. James, sitting inside a friend's house at the semi-formal after-party was excited when he answered. Gail was reluctant to break the news to him in that moment but when he insisted on staying the night at his friend's house, she had to tell him why he couldn't. She heard him gasp in shock. He agreed to come home straight away.

Chris was breathing deeply as the sedative took effect, safe in the hands of his hospital and resigned to the stillness of the moment. But Gail was slipping into shock. Her mind raced to practical details: the mortgage, the practice, leased cars, school fees. Chris's employees. His patients! So many people were relying on him. No sick leave, redundancy or bonus. No partner or structure to absorb the work or clean up after him. Besides, their wonderful life together seemed to be imploding, but Gail couldn't understand this yet. Her mouth was dry and she was pacing back and forth, up and down again and again in the small cubicle. 'Would you like to sit down?' a sweet nurse asked. Gail couldn't have done that, even if she had wanted to. Her heart was pounding through her chest and her throat was burning.

Professor Michael Besser arrived. He had already seen the CT scans and heard the news. He was regarded by many, including Chris, as the best neurosurgeon in the country. He spoke to Chris surgeon-to-surgeon. 'Chris, it's bad,' he said. 'It's a glioma. The best is six to twelve months.'

Gail watched them talk and their voices melted to silence. In that situation some people might have asked a thousand questions, trying to get all the information possible and make sense of it all. But the news was so bad that Gail went the other way. She recoiled from it, withdrawing into herself. She crouched down by the wall and held her head, rocking back and forth.

Michael knelt beside her, reached out and touched her hand. Gail lifted her head. He looked at her gently, his eyes saying everything his words could not. Gail still remembers this tender, compassionate moment. Michael had talked colleague-to-colleague with Chris. He hadn't minced words or tried to hide the truth. All he could do for Gail in this moment was touch her hand and look into her eyes. That's what he did, and for that she is still grateful.

Chris was put on a drip of steroids to reduce the swelling in his brain and admitted into the intensive care unit. Over the next few days we would discover the answers to the health issues of those past few perplexing weeks. As the cancerous cells inside his brain multiplied rapidly, nearby blood vessels were releasing fluids that supplied an army of white blood cells to the surrounding tissue. The extra fluid was building until the immense pressure inside Chris's skull made him feel his head was about to explode. Twenty-four hours later he would have been unconscious; had the intracranial pressure reached this level a few weeks earlier Chris might have been alone in a hotel room in Cleveland, Ohio, or on a plane over the Pacific Ocean.

The pressure extended to his brain stem, which had caused the vomiting, and was centred behind his right eye, pushing it to droop. It caused a large blind spot in the lower left quadrant of his left eye, which explained why he had kept hitting the left-hand gutter that night in Paddington.

There was a long list of symptoms, and the question might arise: why didn't Chris suspect sooner that something was so wrong? He was a doctor, wasn't he? But the dots hadn't been connected. They just didn't know what they didn't know.

Meeting Despair

When we arrived home late that first night, Luc, Michèle and Gareth made us something to eat as James and I sat quietly at the kitchen bench. My mother had people around her, yet she felt like she was alone at the bottom of an abyss. She had to decide when and how to spread the news. Chris's brother, Mike, and sister, Carmel, needed to be told. Gail desperately wanted to call her sister-in-law as Carmel and her husband, Phil, were pillars of family support. But Gail decided to tell them, and others, the following day. *Let everyone have one more night in the world as it was*, she thought.

Gail lay alone in bed and at some point crashed into an exhausted sleep. At about six the next morning, she blinked open her eyes and ever so briefly forgot about the events of the night before. She turned her head and saw the place where Chris should have been and everything flooded back. Instead of waking from a nightmare, she woke into one.

While James and I slept, Gail got up and padded downstairs. Luc was in the kitchen unpacking the dishwasher. He told her that he planned to drive to Goulburn to bring Adam home. Gail was grateful that Luc and Michèle were there. She roused our old dog and took him out for a walk. Woolwich Road was the same as ever on this Sunday morning, one of spring's final flourishes before summer crowded it out. The day was ready to sparkle as the sun quickly rose into the sky with the background sound of birds singing. The occasional car passed. 'Good morning!' a neighbour called out. Gail looked around at the scene which was so familiar yet somehow changed. She was dressed in light clothes but felt as though a lead cloak was hanging over her shoulders. She trudged along, concentrating on the concrete and placing one foot in front of the other.

When she arrived home she phoned Carmel and gave her the news, saying she hadn't called earlier because she hadn't wanted to give Carmel and Phil a sleepless night. Gail then called her parents and some close friends.

Next, she looked up the number of their financial adviser, Noelene Watson, a terrier-like woman who could always be relied upon for incisive advice. Noelene's bluntness had matched Chris's five years before when she had told Gail and Chris that they needed to take out risk insurance. 'Well, how much is that going to cost?' Chris had asked, while Gail cringed. He could be embarrassingly rude at times, she thought. But Noelene hadn't backed off. 'Chris. This is what you need. If something happens to you, what's Gail going to do? How are the kids going to stay in their schools and you all stay in this house?' Chris had given in; Gail would file the insurance bills away before he saw them so he wouldn't change his mind. One evening she accidentally left an invoice on the kitchen bench and he spotted it. 'Look at this! I'm out there working like a slave so you can all live like millionaires when I'm dead and gone. I'm going to call Noelene tomorrow.' Mum had looked at me and rolled her eyes; it was difficult to tell whether or not he was joking. Luckily, he hadn't made that call. Now it already seemed that the advice had been prescient. Gail spoke to Noelene, who immediately said that she would look into their financial options and insurance entitlements.

By this time, James and I had already returned to Dad's bedside at RPA. Gail got changed and followed. When she walked into the neurosurgical intensive care ward, Chris was sitting up in bed. The intravenous steroids had acted swiftly, he had slept soundly and woken refreshed and headache-free. He was wearing a hospital gown but looked anything but sick. His muscular legs were stretched out and crossed over one another. His strong arms and hands were gesticulating as he talked on his mobile phone. He had sent a group text message to dozens of people: 'I've been diagnosed with a malignant brain tumour and will have surgery soon. I expect to do well and will keep you informed. Cheers, Chris.' The message had prompted concerned phone calls and texts, which he was now fielding.

His black hair was as rich as ever; he had good colour in his face. He seemed fine! Not unwell at all. Gail nestled into his neck, feeling his resonant voice reverberate through his throat. She ran her hands through his hair and looked at him in disbelief. He was the same. Surely there had been some mistake.

When more family and friends began to arrive and crowded around the bed, Gail stood back and watched. Carmel, ever attentive to people around her and family needs, put her hand on Gail's shoulder. 'Let's go and get a coffee.' They climbed the stairs in RPA's vast atrium that was flooded with daylight, towards the hospital's Jacaranda Café. They chose a table outside amidst a wash of purple flowers. Carmel went to the counter to order and Gail sat alone for a minute. She felt the black cloak weigh her down and bent her head, covered her face with her hands and broke down.

Carmel came and sat beside her.

'I don't think I can do this,' Gail said. 'I can't. I can't do this.'

Carmel rubbed her back. She did not need to ask what my mother meant. But years later I did.

'To watch him die,' my mother told me. 'I could not watch him die.'

The next day Chris came home. Our house was being flooded with flowers and cards and there were constant phone calls and emails. The perfume of oriental lilies enveloped the place. There were so many fruit baskets that we had fruit flies.

Guillaume Brahimi visited with a box from Guillaume at Bennelong, his wonderful Opera House restaurant. Guillaume had become a dear friend of Chris's since being recruited onto the board of the Sydney Cancer Centre Foundation. Big and burly with a sweet temperament and playful smile, Guillaume was clearly as fond of Chris as Chris was of him. After Dad's diagnosis I would hear him say at the end of phone conversations with Gui, 'I love you too, mate.'

'All you 'ave to do is drop these into boiling water,' Guillaume said, standing at our kitchen bench and holding up duck and jus in a sealed plastic bag. 'And here is some of my Paris mash, which just needs reheating.' Then he presented us with a chocolate tart as big as a bicycle wheel and two bottles of wine — a 1986 Échezeaux from Burgundy and an '82 Château Haut-Brion from Bordeaux. Guillaume has said that sitting down together and breaking bread as a family is a nourishing tonic, especially in a time of crisis. He was right. Eating that buttery mashed potato and succulent duck (it was the best meal I've ever cooked), we basked in each other's company and took more pleasure than ever in the immediate moment.

Friends held down the fort, shopping, cooking, running errands, relieving Gail to some extent of the 'burdensome sea anchor of domestic duties', as Chris once said. The heavy knocker on the front door echoed through the hallway repeatedly, ushering in more family and friends, who stayed and surrounded us.

Chris responded so well to the steroids that it was hard to believe how sick he had been. He and Gail went back to RPA for MRI and PET scans. Again, Gail choked up as she watched Chris's body slide unresisting into the huge metallic mouth of the machine. She left for the chemist to pick up medication to stop stomach ulceration and bleeding from the oral steroids Chris was taking. As she walked up Missenden Road, she spotted Michael Besser coming towards her. *This is it*, she thought. *He's going to tell me it will all be all right. That there's no reason to cry. That it's not as bad as we thought.*

'Chris is having his scans?' Michael asked.

'Yes,' she said. 'Michael, can he be cured?'

Again he looked into her eyes with a compassion that said he wished it were not so, but an unflinching gaze that said he could not alter reality. 'No, Gail.'

She looked across Missenden Road and into the distance. 'But ... but he's so magnificent,' she said, partly to herself.

'Yes, he is. He is magnificent.'

She looked back at him. Their eyes filled with tears.

The next day Gail and Chris went to Professor Besser's rooms. He put the scans up on a screen so the light behind shone through and illuminated images of Chris's brain. It showed a tumour about three centimetres in diameter lying slightly above and behind his right ear. Close by were two smaller nodules known as satellite tumours.

Chris said what Gail wanted to hear. 'I know this tumour has a bad reputation but I want you to do your best to fix me. I want to be cured.'

'Chris, I can operate on you but you won't be cured, not with those satellites there.'

Chris instantly revised his wish: 'I'd really just like to get next year.' James would turn eighteen and sit for his Higher School Certificate.

'You will get next year,' Michael said. Then later he volunteered, 'If you want to, you could get a second opinion.' They said they didn't want to. They trusted him implicitly.

Chris knew enough about glioblastoma multiforme, which has one of the worst survival rates among all human cancers. Its malignancy comes from its tendency to spread its cells aggressively like a spider's web, planting more satellite tumours around itself; this web-like formation makes it impossible to completely extract and it is near inevitably lethal. The median survival time after diagnosis is in the range of twelve months. Patients who live more than three years are considered long-term survivors.

'What a thing to get,' Chris said in disbelief.

'It's not a bad way to go,' Michael offered. Not surprisingly, Chris didn't find this reassuring at all.

Michael Besser explained that Chris would need to continue taking medication to keep the cranial swelling at bay, as well as anti-seizure medication. Chris would never be able to drive again. To preserve his quality of life, Professor Besser would not seek to remove the entire tumour in the operation; he would remove the main mass, but the satellites would remain. As they made their way through the corridors, lifts and car park, my mother quietly sobbed. He was fifty-four years old and she fifty-two. How transient our happiness had been.

That night, they lay together in each other's arms.

'Tough week,' Chris stated.

'We just have to grind through this. That's all we can do.'

Brain Surgery

Dad looked cosy in a navy blue jumper on the day he was to undergo brain surgery on 30 November 2006 — five days after his diagnosis in emergency. James was at school and Adam had returned to Goulburn. The roads were quiet as Dad, Mum and I drove to the hospital at seven o'clock. On previous early morning drives with Dad, he would flick between radio stations in order to capture a cross-section of news and opinions of the day. (Even the way he listened to the radio was efficient.) But on this day he didn't turn the radio on. We listened to the hum of the engine as Mum on autopilot guided the car towards Royal Prince Alfred Hospital.

The perioperative room was small and dark. I could see that the nurse's light-hearted chatter tired Gail, but she smiled and politely responded to questions. When we were left alone, Chris sat on the edge of the bed, closed his eyes and breathed deeply and rhythmically.

'Hello!' Dr Anthony Durrell, a psychiatrist a few years my father's junior at medical school, appeared in the doorway. Wearing a straw fedora and holding a long, painted canvas in front of him, he was not someone we expected to see in this place and moment. Dad seemed pleased by the distraction.

'I thought I'd come and catch you. I brought this.' He held up the painting, which was his own work. It showed a vibrant pattern of colours, depicting four quadrants. As he explained how the quadrants represented moods of fear, anger, sadness and happiness, I looked at my mother. She seemed oblivious to the conversation and was looking down at her hands holding Dad's phone and watch.

It wasn't long before Dad was lying on the trolley that would take him into surgery. Wearing a hospital gown and with his hair under a cap, he pulled Gail close as she blinked back tears. He caressed her cheek, then mine, smiled at us both, and was wheeled away.

'I don't know how anyone does this with television cameras watching,' Mum said as we trudged upstairs to the café. She was referring to all the RPA patients who had agreed to let Channel 9 cameras film them during these moments. We took a table outside where the air was warm and fragrant with the smell of jacarandas. Mum looked depleted but appeared to be holding up. She walked to the counter to buy coffees. When she got back to the table, she found me bawling and her strength seeped away. She hugged me close to her chest and sat on the chair beside me.

The tears streamed down her face like rain on a window. Over the coming years, my mother's strong exterior would often be overpowered by the sight of one of her children crying. 'I need to go to uni to finish a group assignment,' I eventually told her, and she agreed that it would be easier if we were not together. Gail drove down to the southern suburb of Caringbah and spent the morning at her parents' house. Being with her mother and father, she felt lighter and cheerier. When Dr Besser rang to say that the surgery had gone very well, she was elated. Adam, James and I breathed sighs of relief as she relayed the report to each of us over the phone. We didn't know what the future held but at least it was hopeful in a momentary way.

When I returned to the neurosurgical intensive care unit, Mum and James were already there. Dad was propped up in bed with a white bandage wrapped around his head. He gulped down two cartons of cold chocolate milk through a straw as Mum held them for him. Later, he ate tasty salt and pepper prawns that James and I had gone out and bought.

After taking a long sip of the cold, sweet milk, he leaned his head back and closed his eyes. 'Why did you get this brain tumour, Dad?' James asked.

'Being completely overworked,' Mum said. 'That's what did this to him.'

Dad smiled without opening his eyes. He said, 'In the main hospital foyer downstairs, there's a stained-glass window with the inscription, *Mortalibus non arduum*. Hard work never killed anyone.'

Chris's mobile phone rang and Gail answered it for him. She covered the receiver. 'It's Frank Sartor. He wants to know how you are.' Sartor was the New South Wales assistant minister for health (cancer) by that stage, and he and Dad had come to know and like each other. 'Tell Frank I'm going into politics now I've only got half a brain,' Chris said from his pillow. Frank's laugh cracked through the phone's speaker. We heard him say, 'We need you, Chris.' Mum laughed too; Dad seemed so well.

James reminded us that *RPA* was on television that night. Dad was likely to be on it, having been filmed recently treating a young woman for a benign tumour in her neck. We turned it on and increased the volume on the patient audio handset to maximum. If we all gathered around it at the head of the bed, we could just make out the tinny sound coming out of the speaker. There we were crowding around Dad as he lay on a hospital bed in RPA with his head extravagantly bandaged, watching him in his familiar role as surgeon in the same institution. At the end of the program the familiar voice of Max Cullen announced that Professor Chris O'Brien had been diagnosed with a brain tumour and had undergone surgery earlier that day. 'We wish him well with his treatment,' he added. We were later told that this announcement had prompted the hospital switchboards to light up as viewers rang to ask if they'd heard the announcement correctly, and to convey their shock and concern. We could see how completely he had captured people's hearts and attention. This was the first step in his journey becoming public.

We stayed together for a while longer with Dad resting his head against the pillow. Mum asked whether he was warm enough and arranged his pyjamas, phone, toiletries and other belongings in the cupboard and on the bedside table. I perched on the edge of the bed.

Dad started to tell us the story about when James was born. 'You know, when Jamie was so sick, and it didn't look like he was going to survive, Carmel came with me to mass just up the road here,' he said. 'We went in and I looked up. There was a big banner hanging at the front with gold letters.' His eyes looked beyond me and his hand glided through the air. 'It said "He Lives." His voice cracked and his face crumpled and he wept ever so briefly. Adam, James and I had never heard this story before. How potent the memory must have been for it to stir this emotion in my father at this moment.

Dad stayed in hospital for three days, while a parade of people shuffled through the door to his room. When we were there we wheeled him outside for fresh air. As he sat in a wheelchair, wearing his pyjamas, he closed his eyes and offered his face to the warm sunshine and gentle breeze.

Back at home, my mother was wrestling with the practical implications of Dad's diagnosis. She decided to contract everything. Rein it all in. It was as if we were expecting a blizzard and needed to bring everything inside. She cancelled credit cards and talked about getting rid of one or two cars; the family had four at the time. The study was swamped with paperwork as she tracked our outgoings: leases, bills, James's school fees, a weekly gardener and cleaner. Then there were Chris's consulting rooms with rent, staff, insurance, other bills. The phone rang constantly and people were forever knocking on the door. It was the beginning of a tidal wave of love and support that would sustain us for years to come, but life was busy and chaotic.

I escaped the frenzy at home by spending as much time at the hospital as I could. I was lucky to have been able to clear my days, with university over and the flexibility to rearrange shifts at my casual jobs. James had one more week of school term, and Adam's training in Goulburn only allowed for a short break over Christmas as he worked towards graduation only a few months away. On those hot December days, I sat by Dad in his cool, dim room. I enjoyed the quiet moments when they came, listening to Dad's deep, rhythmic breathing as he napped, attempting the *Herald* crossword and watching the Australian cricket team wallop the Poms. I had found myself a still and peaceful place that offered nourishment, which my mother could not afford to seek. I knew little of the torrent of problems that raced through her mind day and night.

Dad was eager to come home. He couldn't rest well in hospital and the one time he had managed to fall into a deep sleep he was woken by a nurse concerned by his heart rate slowing down to forty beats per minute, when, in fact, that was the resting rate of his big, strong heart.

When Dad was to be brought home, I felt frustrated with my mother as I peered through the study doorway and found her sitting in front of the computer. 'Mum, what are you doing?'

She looked over her shoulder, tired and frowning. 'I'm just trying to put the Volvo up for sale.'

'Why do you have to do that *now*?'

She sighed loudly, 'I just need to get some things done before he gets home.'

'We can do that later, Mum, Dad's waiting for us.'

She stood up and walked past me. 'All right, let's just go.'

We double-parked in a small lot in front of the hospital and followed the corridors to intensive care. Dad was dressed, packed and ready to leave. I knew he would be annoyed at having had to wait so long, and he was.

'I thought you were coming this morning.'

'Christie, it has been frantic with the phone ringing and people everywhere. I've had so much to do.'

For the first time his wound wasn't covered. It was a long gash about ten centimetres on the right side of his head with more than a dozen black staples pulling the skin tautly together. We carried his bag to the car and drove home in silence.

The second night he was home, Gail woke to find Chris in a highly agitated state. Anxiety combined with steroid-induced hyperactivity was making his mind a chaotic whirlpool of dark thoughts and fears. They went downstairs, sat in the study and discussed Gail's future life as a widow. She said she couldn't and wouldn't go on, and cried floods of desperate tears. Chris shed some of his own. For almost thirty years they had been together in everything and now they were together facing something that was bigger than both of them.

Then, as Dad would describe it, they slowly fought their way to the front of this runaway train, trying to grasp the controls and at least bring some certainty to their domestic circumstances. They wanted control and control meant maths. They calculated Chris's superannuation and the insurance payments. The business expense insurance wasn't enough to cover the ongoing costs of the practice. That could be supplemented with the income protection insurance, but they still had to pay the mortgage as well as myriad other costs. Gail said she could return to practising as a physiotherapist. But it seemed unavoidable that we would have to sell our home. She suggested that they inspect a smaller house for sale nearby. The unspoken rationale was that it would be a more appropriate size to accommodate Gail as a widow.

The next morning, Gail called the estate agent and arranged an immediate inspection of the neighbour's house. They walked through the small, pretty rooms, envisaging their own furniture, paintings and belongings in them. It was being rented by two teenage schoolboys who went to Riverview, the private school that Adam had attended and James still did. The pair recognised Chris and Gail.

'G'day, boys,' Chris said casually. Gail was conscious of the large gash and sutures on the side of Chris's head with the surrounding hair shaved. She thought she saw one of the boys eye the wound and felt awkward; here was a senior surgeon inspecting a house that two teenagers were living in. The image Chris and Gail presented to the outside world was being transformed.

Finding Hope

The post-surgical plan was for Chris to begin radiotherapy and chemotherapy concurrently. The chemo would be taken orally first thing in the morning on an empty stomach. The radiotherapy would involve his head being fitted into a fibreglass mask bolted to a treatment table so he would be completely immobilised, allowing the radiation machine to target the tumour with pinpoint precision. The mask needed to be moulded to the shape of his face and head, and an appointment was scheduled at radiation oncology in the first week of December.

On a sunny midweek morning, Gail parked her car outside the building where she had spent much of her final two years of physio study. The radiation oncology unit was lively and bustling with staff and patients. Professor Chris Milross, the head of the department and close friend of my parents, greeted them with characteristic warmth but unfamiliar concern. The three of them chatted about the diagnosis quietly, before he summed it up. 'Fuck,' he exhaled.

Dr George Hruby, a senior radiation oncologist, took Chris and Gail into a separate room for the consultation. After discussing the treatment plan, George looked Chris straight in the eyes. 'We're going to go after this, Chris,' he said. This attitude was reinforced by Professor Brian McCaughan. A cardiothoracic surgeon at RPA and long-time friend, Brian listened as Chris told him about the previous days and the poor prognosis he had been handed. 'Well, that's all bullshit and you know it,' Brian asserted. 'Patients decide how long they will live, you know that. Doctors don't decide how long patients have. We've both made that mistake. You just have to decide that you are going to fight this and prove them all wrong.'

For my parents, the impact of these words and attitudes was almost immediate. How powerful positive reinforcement can be. Absolutely nothing had changed about the circumstances or Chris's prognosis. Yet George Hruby's and Brian McCaughan's defiance and encouragement were compelling. It was as if Chris and Gail had just swallowed a pill that helped them to think clearly and optimistically.

Later, Noelene visited with details of how the insurance and finance safety nets would work. The good news was that the income protection would indeed allow us to keep the house.

The tide of desperation was rolling back. What they now needed was deep, restful sleep and more than a week after the operation and more than two weeks after the diagnosis, they finally managed to get that. The healing and nurturing effects of sleep worked to buoy their spirits and thoughts.

Invariably, the medical literature about glioblastoma multiforme contains a terrifying graph that depicts patient survival rates. Along the y-axis is the number of patients still alive, and along the x-axis is time. As the curve moves from left to right, it plunges from high to low. It sweeps through milestones — three months since diagnosis, six months, one year, two years — falling towards the x-axis and illustrating fewer and fewer survivors. The curve falls to a place just above the straight black line. But it never quite reaches it. A small gap remains between the curve and the axis. This is where hope lives.

Against all the odds, Christmas 2006 was one of our most joyous. For as long as I remember we have spent Christmas Eve with my father's side of the family. This year we were joined by Mum's parents and a wonderfully eclectic group of Dad's colleagues, his fellow radiotherapy patients and other orphans and blow-ins. Jatin Shah, the leading head and neck surgeon at Memorial Sloan Kettering Cancer Center in New York City, had flown from the USA to spend the afternoon and evening with us. Our neighbour Col Joye, who announces himself on the phone by saying, 'G'day, sweetheart, Col Joye of the Joy Boys, from down the hill', regaled us with stories and songs on his ukulele.

The lounge room doors opened onto the lush garden, towering hedges and tinkling fountain. We peeled prawns in the kitchen and drank wine and tea by sprawling wisteria and bougainvillea, overlooking the beautiful river. Mum's father swam gentle laps in the pool as James back-flipped and bombed into the water around him. Our little old dog, a miniature schnauzer named Mr Menzies because of his bushy eyebrows (Dad's idea), raced up and down barking at the splashes. Adam, our cousin Matthew and Gareth sat on and stood beside a weathered cane sofa next to the pool. The house was full of people, sound and activity. In the middle of it all was Dad. Wearing just his Speedos and straw hat, he was sprawled on a wooden sun lounge. He smiled at me and raised his cup of tea in one hand and plate of cake in the other. 'It doesn't get much better than this,' he said.

Mum was inside, sitting on a kitchen stool near the open French windows. She wore no make-up, light blue shorts and a white T-shirt. She was on the phone to somebody, talking about the treatment procedures and plans. Her previous moribund, fatalistic attitude had faded. She was speaking about the next steps — radiotherapy, chemotherapy, another scan in a month.

We had survived those short painful weeks between the diagnosis on 25 November and Christmas Eve. We had fallen to the depths of despair but now we were pulling ourselves back up to a place of hope.

* * *

Then came the practical realities and ordeals of life as a cancer patient. Dad started on oral chemotherapy which, with anti-seizure medication, made him terribly nauseated and gave everything a foul, metallic taste so that even drinking water was almost intolerable. His daily radiotherapy appointments were scheduled for first thing in the morning — an attempt by the radiotherapy staff to ensure that he wouldn't have to wait in the waiting room but which forced him and Mum into negotiating congested peak-hour traffic. When he arrived, he would lie down on the treatment table and the rigid fibreglass mask would be placed over his head and bolted to a frame, the facial equivalent of a straitjacket.

As the treatment continued, his nausea worsened. It was January and the hospital was quiet, with many staff and doctors away on holidays. Not able to keep food or liquid down, he became depleted and started shedding weight. He saw a hospital dietician but was left disappointed with the solution: a supplement formula that tasted like chocolate- or banana-flavoured puke, as he described it. He couldn't eat or drink, and there didn't seem to be anyone to help him.

Fortunately one oncology professor, Martin Tattersall, had not gone on holidays. He said Chris was desperately dehydrated, admitted him to hospital and put him on a drip. Two litres of water with salts flowed into Chris's veins and were absorbed into his body. Blood tests revealed that his liver function was abnormal. Gail phoned her father and told him about the liver function test. Murray said that the anti-epilepsy pills Chris was taking would affect his liver, and added that Chris needed to drink plenty of water. Gail hung up, relieved. Her father's advice was always well informed, straightforward and immediate. Even though my parents had unfettered access to scores of medical contacts, Murray's help was indispensable. *How do people cope without all of this inside knowledge?* she wondered.

Chris focused on drinking plenty of water and a dash of ginger cordial made it palatable enough. He still wasn't able to eat much, and what he did eat frequently came up again. During the night, Gail would listen to him in the bathroom being sick. Back in bed she would stroke his hair as she had always done. But his hair was now coming out in her fingers and onto the pillow, not from the chemotherapy but from the radiation being beamed through his scalp. A large patch of bald head became obvious so Chris had his head shaved. Gail scooped up some of his thick black hair and placed it in a precious box in her bedside table.

He continued to shed weight and started to lose his strong, robust physique. But despite all of this, his attitude remained stoic and realistic. When someone asked, 'Why has this happened to you?', his response was, 'Why not me?' He met each indignity with humour, finding comedy in even the darkest and most difficult times. He would tell people that early morning radiotherapy appointments left the remainder of the day for leisure activities like vomiting and sleeping, or say that having retired, his days were now spent looking for his glasses and battling constipation (another uncomfortable side effect of the medication). He wryly quipped that overwhelming nausea during radiotherapy sessions — in which his head was confined to a position looking up at the ceiling — made him scared that he would 'die like a rock star' by drowning in his own vomit. 'Nothing cures nausea like a good chuck,' he once said cheerily after emerging from the bathroom. Another favourite line was, 'The first thing I do in the morning is wake up and check my pulse to make sure I'm still alive.'

The opportunity to make memories is the blessing of a forecasted death, as opposed to a sudden one. With Dad now constantly around and physically well most of the time, our days were filled with happiness and freedom. In some ways, life was even better than it had been before. My clearest memories are of the simplest moments. Dad and I would do the newspaper crossword in the morning and walk to a local café in the afternoon. As summer became autumn and the air grew chilly, the café provided red throws for guests to drape discreetly over their knees. Dad hung a blanket over his head like a hijab and I giggled to see our teenage waiter do a double-take as he put the coffees down. Dad decided my brothers and I had to learn to drive manual cars, saying, 'It's a life skill you've got to have,' and determinedly taught us despite much whingeing and resistance from the three of us. He was more fun and more irreverent than ever. One afternoon, James and Dad walked to the park with our little dog trailing after them. Mr Menzies, old and mature enough not to be walked on a lead, relieved himself on a nature strip as Dad and James walked on. They heard a woman call out behind them. 'Excuse me! Your dog did a poo back there!'

'Well, did you pick it up?' Dad answered.

But for all our joy, we could never escape the sense that we were tied to train tracks, powerless to stop an oncoming locomotive. My mother had a horrifying dream of a dark, murky, menacing cloud appearing at their bedroom door. Billowing and heaving, it passed around Chris and floated towards her, threatening to engulf her whole. She tried to fight it off, beating it with her fists. It disappeared just as suddenly as it had come. Her thrashing had woken Chris, and as he whispered to her in the darkness, she came to consciousness. The dream was an intuition of our lives, in which we were constantly keeping one step ahead of death, constantly fighting it off.

Each month Chris would have a scan to monitor the effect of the treatment. The main mass had been debulked in the first operation and the hope was that it had not recurred and the concurrent therapies would take care of the satellites. These scans would approach with a crescendo of anxiety. We would collectively hold our breaths until Dad had viewed the results, which he was able to do immediately with the medical imaging director. No recurrence or growth would be met with an exhalation of relief, but inevitably the month came when the scan revealed bad news. In April it showed that the main tumour mass had regrown and a satellite was enlarged. This diabolical disease was demonstrating that its notoriety had been well earned. It was five months since that night in RPA's emergency ward when Michael Besser predicted that Chris would have between six and twelve months to live. His prophecy was coming true, exactly as he said it would. And we were not ready.

After this news my parents attended mass, which they were doing more frequently these days. Gail had converted to Catholicism in 2000 and usually took great comfort in the community atmosphere of the parish. But as she sat in a pew, she felt the walls of the church close in on her. She excused herself and edged along the row, her vision blurred from the welling tears. She rushed outside and stood in the building's shadow, unable to catch her breath, sobbing into her hands. Chris had followed her out; there was nothing he could do or say. He just wrapped his arms around her and they stood locked together.

Several people had suggested that Dad see Dr Charlie Teo for a second opinion. Charlie, a high-profile neurosurgeon adored by the public but cast as something of a maverick by the medical fraternity, was known for his brilliance and willingness to pursue aggressive surgical treatment. Chris knew Charlie from the beginning of their careers; even as a neurosurgical registrar Charlie had had a reputation for being as flamboyant as he was gifted and hard-working.

Chris had reservations. He was loyal to Michael Besser and trusted his advice. Also, seeing Charlie would mean being treated at Prince of Wales Hospital, a peripheral consideration but one that required a shift in thinking for an RPA man. Gail said she would support Chris in whatever he chose. But ultimately, the choice was not between Michael Besser or Charlie Teo. Nor was it a question of Royal Prince Alfred Hospital or Prince of Wales. The choice was between succumbing to what seemed inevitable or pursuing what might be possible. Would he be a passive patient, accepting of his fate, or a proactive advocate, rejecting foregone conclusions? Would he choose life, or would he say die?

To Choose Life

Chris and Gail sat in Dr Teo's office on a Saturday morning. Charlie bowled in, wearing a grey T-shirt, blue jeans and carrying a motorcycle helmet. His head was shaved like Chris's, though for a different reason entirely. He exuded confidence and looked so youthful. Gail had never seen a surgeon like him.

Charlie held the scans up to the window and looked into them quickly, with almost a cursory glance. He said he was confident that he could do something with fairly low risk and went on to explain that the plan would be to debulk the tumour and radically remove a lot of surrounding tissue.

This was the moment Gail had been waiting for. They were still in the game.

Chris approached the operation with a matter-of-fact, job-to-be-done attitude. On the day of the operation, James accompanied our parents to Prince of Wales Hospital. This time, however, they were joined by a television camera crew as well. *60 Minutes* had begun doing a story about Dad, which meant that Gail had reluctantly agreed to have cameras present. But she was pleased to find that they were not invasive or disruptive at all. The reporter, Peter Overton, was a warm, loving man who quickly became a friend to the whole family. The crew were forever sensitive and diplomatic. People have often asked whether the media coverage was an intrusion. Mum, Adam and I felt as though it was the opposite: Peter Overton and the crew were almost a support team who would intermittently appear in our lives. But I know that James would have preferred to be without it.

Charlie emerged from surgery to tell Gail and James that the operation was a great success. He had been very aggressive in his interventions and already checked Chris's movement. No disability was evident.

Two days later, a nurse stood at the foot of Dad's bed in Prince of Wales Hospital.

'Have you moved your bowels today, Professor O'Brien?' she asked.

'No. Have you?' He was discharged that day.

Home again, Dad began a new concoction of chemotherapy administered by his new neuro-oncologist, Dr Helen Wheeler. Initially after diagnosis, Chris had asked Dr Michael Boyer, head of medical oncology and then acting director of the Sydney Cancer Centre, to supervise his care. But Dr Boyer's expertise lay in lung and prostate cancers and so, on Michael's recommendation, Chris sought the advice of Dr Wheeler.

Caring, highly intelligent and relentless in her approach to the treatment of brain tumours, Chris and Gail had full confidence in Helen Wheeler. When they first met her, she had her arm in plaster after tripping over her dog down the stairs, giving her an absent-minded-professor kind of quality.

Just six weeks later it became clear that the operation had not been enough. The largest satellite tumour was proving resistant to the chemo, and it was growing. Charlie Teo and Michael Besser had both warned Chris that removing this tumour posed the most serious risks. Located in the brain stem, it required opening one of the fluid cavities to the brain, with the risk of spilling malignant cells down the spinal column. More likely, even inevitably, was the prospect that Chris would be left with a hemiparesis (weakness down an entire side of the body) and hemianopia (loss of the visual field on one side). The tumour was on his right side, and any ill effects would be on his left. Charlie repeated the warnings, but Chris asked him to do whatever was necessary to remove that remaining tumour satellite and make him as disease-free as possible. Chris believed in his own profession's capacity to give him the best chance of survival. He was prepared to face the risks, because he had already faced the crossroads. He had chosen life. And this was the path to which his choice led.

Gail was beside Chris when he woke from the anaesthetic after his third operation. They were in a neat room at Prince of Wales Hospital with a carpeted floor and bare walls. Chris's body was propped upright in the raised bed. He blinked as he opened his eyes. 'Oh,' he said gently. 'I've got the hemianopia.' He turned his head slightly and looked in front of him, lifted his right arm and moved it in front of his face in a wide arc.

'I can't see anything from here onwards.' He motioned from a line that started just to the left of his eyes and moved outwards.

He started to peel off his covers and clumsily moved his legs to the side of the bed. Gail jumped to his side and held his right arm. He stood and tried to take a step with his left foot but it couldn't find the floor and pedalled through the air. Gail quickly moved around to his unsupported left side. His left arm was hooked close to his chest with his hand and fingers stiff and contorted. She bent down, took his left calf and ankle between her hands and placed his foot on the floor, stood up and resumed carrying his weight. He took a step with his right foot, then lifted his left, and again it swung and jerked without finding solid ground. Gail repeated what she'd done before.

'Looks like I've got a bit of a hemiparesis as well,' he said. They turned around and he leaned heavily on her as they stumbled the few steps back to the bed. She helped him slide himself onto it and lifted his left leg in. She went to the foot of the bed and placed her hand under the sole of his left foot.

'Can you push against my hand?' she asked, the first time she had used her knowledge in neurophysiotherapy for decades. After a couple of seconds he was able to awkwardly push his left foot forward.

It was late when she left and Chris was drifting in and out of sleep. She was exhausted and he told her she should go home. She kissed him and said she would be back first thing in the morning. She pulled the door to his room closed and let it click shut, before standing still for a moment on her own. She took a huge, deep breath and raised her eyes to the ceiling. What trauma had occurred in his brain, his magnificent brain? *How will he cope tonight without me?* She assured herself that the nursing staff would make sure he was okay, and kept walking.

Chris had a bad night. His left side was too weak for him to get out of bed on his own. He had to use the toilet but was so paralysed he couldn't reach for the buzzer dangling over the left side of the bed. He was forced to lie and wait for the next time somebody came to check on him. When Gail arrived the next morning, his bedsheets were crumpled and askew under his body. His pillow had slid away from under his head. He needed a shave and a shower and she asked someone to help her.

Gail got him cleaned up but was concerned about the next two nights. He was so disabled that he needed to be looked after minute by minute, and Gail, exhausted herself, couldn't be there all the time. She called her old friend Jenny, who convinced her to get a special nurse; it had been common for 'specials' to be employed for high-dependency patients at RPA in the 1970s when Jenny and Gail were young physios. Jenny made the arrangements with an agency, and a 'special' came over that day to look after Chris. We heard whispers that the ward and nurse unit manager weren't impressed, believing that 'Mrs O'Brien doesn't think her husband is being looked after well enough'. But Mum didn't give a damn about what anyone thought. All that mattered was that her own arrangements — privately paid for — ensured that Chris had the care he needed.

When Gail arrived with Carmel and Phil to take Chris home, he was ready to leave. He had dressed himself, which had taken him an hour, and managed to fumble most of his shirt buttons through their holes. Gail did up the remaining buttons and helped him lift his blue jumper over his head and push his arms through the sleeves. He looked terrible. He was pale, thin and unable to walk without Phil bearing most of his weight.

They had been told that the first few days would be the worst. The swelling from the operation made the hemiplegia stronger but his movement would improve as the swelling reduced. Chris lay in bed, unable to move much at all. The loss of the left half of his visual field made reading difficult too.

James was still boarding at school, doing his best to battle through his HSC year. Adam was working in the security industry which required long hours and shift work. I was travelling in Europe with Gareth. We had planned to go overseas but after Dad's diagnosis I was reluctant to leave. Dad insisted that we go, so we shortened our trip to two months. At the departure gate I had kept on turning around as I walked away and Dad had placed his hand on his heart. I turned the corner and dissolved into tears. It was so hard to go; almost harder than I could bear. If I could advise my younger self now, I think I would say, 'The Louvre isn't going anywhere. What can you see in all those monuments and artworks that could be more wonderful than the love between you and your father? What greater lesson can you learn in Europe than what you can learn at home? Stay with your father. He won't be around for much longer. Wring out every last drop of time with him that you can.'

Lying there in bed after the third operation, alone and unable to move, my father began to cry. Gail heard him and ran in. He didn't stop, just sobbed and sobbed desperate and raw tears, engulfed by helplessness and the inescapable reality of what he had been reduced to. Gail helped to haul him up and they sat on the edge of the bed. She simply held her beloved in silence. There was nothing she could say or do. She now knew what Michael Besser had wanted to avoid.

Only twice in my life did I see my father really cry and both times, it was like watching a giant fall. The first time was after his mother died. My grandmother Maureen was a strong and charismatic woman, a magnificent school principal with a singing, resonant voice who earned the deep love and admiration of her three children. She sustained the family through tough times in their modest home in the western Sydney suburb of Regents Park. She was sixty-nine years old when she died of ovarian cancer in 1995. As I practised violin, aged eleven, in the annexe to the kitchen, I chose a particularly melancholic tune that rang out across the tiled floors. I looked over my sheet music at my father. Dressed in his work suit, he was leaning back against the kitchen bench. He hung his head and covered his face with an outstretched palm. I saw his shoulders heave up and down. As Mum came to console him I stopped playing and left the room.

The second time was after a friend of mine took his own life at the age of nineteen. Dad felt a deep sorrow for me as I wept for days. One evening he came into my room and sat beside me as I lay on my bed. 'I'm so sorry to see you so sad, my darling,' he said. I told him I couldn't stop thinking of how desperate my friend must have been. As I said this, Dad bent over and put his face in his hands and wept next to my shoulder. I was so taken aback that my own tears stopped. Wanting to comfort him, I patted his back. I didn't understand. I still don't. Perhaps it was his daughter's sadness. Perhaps it was the thought of this poor young man ending his life. Perhaps it was because his working life was full of sorrow as well. It was the first time I had any sense that he was not just my strong, brave dad who solved every problem and knew every answer.

In the days following that third operation, the swelling in my father's head did subside and some movement returned to the left side of his body. Guillaume and David Pohl, one of Dad's oldest friends, came to the house and the pair took him out for a walk. They steadied him along the footpath that now seemed so treacherously uneven. His left leg was uncoordinated and he shuffled along with short steps. But in the few metres covered, he found vast improvement and that afternoon was in a lighter, brighter mood. Gail knew that she needed to help him keep his mental state elevated.

As he adjusted to the hemianopia, Dad was able to read again by shifting his line of vision beyond the left of the page. His head would move left to right as if he was watching a ping-pong match as he drank in literature of all kinds. He clutched the books spastically; dozens of paperbacks on our shelves still bear a thick crease down the middle from where his clumsy hand contorted them.

Adam spent a lot of time with Dad at home and James was there every weekend. When Gareth and I arrived back in Australia, we were eager to see my parents. I registered the sight of Mum leading Dad through the crowd at the airport arrivals. He focused on Mum and the path that her hand pulled him along, as her eyes darted around the people and objects in their vicinity, keeping watch for an arm or shoulder that he wouldn't see. He appeared frail. She looked worn. That night at home, we laughed and talked over each other as Gareth and I recounted tales of our trip. We took silly photos with my new camera and relished our reunion. It was so good to be together again.

Sitting in the kitchen at home on my return was more joyous than all the adventures, more wonderful than all the architecture, more inspiring than all the galleries and more nourishing than all the cathedrals that Europe had to offer. We were a family unit fortified by something stronger than steel or iron; we were bolstered by love. Together, we were stronger. And we were all together again.

Caring for
Dr Gorgeous

My father was a loving and appreciative but somewhat demanding dependant. He'd sing out from the office or living room, 'Pinkie?' and if my mother didn't hear the first time, he'd just call a little louder, '*GAIL!*'

Each morning she woke up first to arrange his medications, cut up a small amount of fruit and take everything upstairs to him in bed. He would swallow the pills on an empty stomach and eat the fruit twenty minutes later. By that time Gail would have squeezed a fresh orange juice and be preparing a wholesome breakfast of scrambled eggs, mushrooms and spinach. Through these days, my father was slow to get moving due to medicine-induced fatigue, but once he was up the day seemed to yield little time for Gail. As the nausea had improved, food became a major preoccupation. He was looking forward to meals as a way of breaking up the day and Gail, always keen to make things more bearable, was exploring options that would be palatable and nutritious. Lunch chased down the late breakfast and was quickly followed by afternoon tea, and dinner was preceded by an appetiser. So much of Gail's day was consumed by shopping and preparing meals.

Like a pregnant woman, Chris started to have unusual cravings. One of these was unexpectedly for Malaysian laksa from a small underground canteen at the northern end of Sydney's Queen Victoria Building in the middle of the city — a fifteen-minute drive from home on a good day. With a team of willing drivers, a laksa run became a regular event, where someone would dash into town and bring home bowls of the fragrant soup with noodles and vegetables. The run required logistical planning as there is hardly any street parking around the QVB, so we often made the trip in pairs. On one occasion, Mum drove in by herself and parked illegally for the ten minutes it took to run into the canteen. Her outfit, hardly designed for a dash through the city, featured loose-fitting velvet pants and furry clogs (don't ask). As she galloped down the stairway of the QVB, one of the clogs caught hold of a pant leg and she tumbled down half a flight of stairs. A man coming in the other direction was shocked at this dramatic fall which looked like a racing skier's. But she assured him she was all right, scrambled to her feet and continued down the stairs with her purpose still at the front of her mind. She bought the laksa, made it back to the car (no parking ticket!) and home without further incident. But she had sprained her ankle badly and probably torn a ligament. It's been a weak ankle prone to rolling ever since.

While the sore ankle was inconvenient, Gail didn't mind the pain. In fact, she welcomed it as something real that could be coped with, as opposed to the invisible torture she was suffering. She would spend time in the garden, vigorously pulling at weeds and exerting herself, remaining within earshot of Dad if he should need anything. One day, as she leaned her foot on the edge of a rock and bent forward into a hedge to pull giant weeds from its centre, her foot slipped and her entire shin scraped along the rock's pointed edge. Looking down, she saw her shin was torn from knee to ankle and bleeding profusely. She looked at the sky and said in her mind, *Thank God this is pain I can feel.* Many times, gripped by panic or stress, she would escape the house and sprint down Hunters Hill's main road, running until she felt that her chest was about to explode. Again the painful sensation somehow felt like a release.

Symptoms of her inner torment did outwardly emerge. She was catapulted into menopause earlier than expected. An itchy rash appeared on her left shin, proving resistant to topical creams and medicines. She eventually controlled it with a combination of cortisone cream and oregano oil, but then it moved to her right shin and was even more difficult to treat. Eventually the rash cleared up a year after Chris died.

The focus of the sick is to get better. The focus of the carer is that, plus everything else. While Chris read or snoozed, Gail would race to do grocery shopping and errands. Our house was large and needed a lot of upkeep. The insurance companies required records of profit and loss statements from the practice and current income as invoice payments continued to trickle in. The practice was eventually wound up, a process that Gail oversaw. She would make time for these practicalities late at night, sitting alone in the office tapping into accounting software.

As he used his illness to advocate for better cancer care, Chris was more and more sought after to speak to the media or to take part in cancer fundraising and patient advocacy events. He was completely reliant on Gail to get to many of these. A journalist would come to the house to interview him and unexpectedly ask for a photo of Chris and Gail. For a time, Gail would run upstairs to throw on some make-up. Then she stopped bothering. They could take her as she was. Later she simply said no, she would not be in a photo. Chasing some kind of family element for the picture, photographers often satisfied themselves with the dog accompanying Chris instead.

Adam, now a probationary constable at Newtown Local Area Command, had moved to an apartment in Drummoyne with his girlfriend, Jaya. James was living at home and studying an Arts degree while I (also still at home with Gareth) was working in the media and now studying Graduate Law. We all did our best to support Mum and Dad. But it was clear to me how dependent Dad was on Mum, when he would wonder aloud when she would be home, even though I was being as attentive as I could. He would become anxious that maybe something had happened to her or she was finding it all too hard. The truth is, she rarely took time out for herself because they were in this together. One day, Gail made a long-overdue appointment at her hairdresser. Pam had known Gail for twenty years, from the time I attended the local primary school with her daughter. Pam must have been able to see that her long-time client was exhausted and not herself. She took Gail to the washbasins in the back of the salon, sat her down and placed a towel over her shoulders. As Gail leaned back, she saw that Pam had dimmed the lights. One of the young hairdressers started tenderly massaging Gail's head, and Gail knew the young woman had been told to take extra care of her. Tears welled in her closed eyes and rolled down her temples; this simple act of care for the carer touched her deeply.

Gail was handing Chris fistfuls of pills each day. The latest concoction of medications included temozolomide, procarbazine and thalidomide. She was astonished that he was being given this last drug, like many people associating it with tragic birth defects in babies born in the 1960s whose mothers had taken it for morning sickness. But now thalidomide was being used in trials to treat brain cancer and represented another long shot at survival. As Gail handed these drugs to her husband day after day, she came to look down at the pills in her cupped hand with dread. These medicines were supposed to deal with the malignant cells in his brain, usually by cutting off the blood supply to the tumour. But inevitably they would affect every cell in his body. His skin had taken on a plastic-like sheen and he had developed an eczema-like rash.

Gail began thinking about the impact of everything he was ingesting, not just the toxic chemicals but the food, meats, vegetables, oils, sugars, fats. Having desperately searched for meals he could tolerate during his nausea she had begun to think beyond scrambled eggs, homemade chicken soup and ginger beer — three things that he was able to endure throughout chemo. She researched clinical nutrition in the treatment of cancer, discovering foods that could counteract symptoms and side-effects and maybe even have their own positive therapeutic benefits. She sought out the advice of Dr James Read, a former medical student of Chris's who was now a general practitioner with an encyclopaedic knowledge of nutrition. Other people, friends and strangers alike, sent advice, treatment suggestions and books with titles like *The Ten Best Cancer Cures*. Even a few unpublished manuscripts arrived telling tales of survival and treatment regimes.

Mum had always kept a healthy larder and cooked low-fat meals (forcing Dad, Adam and me to satisfy our sweet-tooth cravings by scoffing white bread lathered in golden syrup). But as my mother's research deepened and she discovered the potential healing powers of nutrition, our fridge and kitchen cupboards became filled with experimental health kick ingredients and supposed super foods.

Many people are vaguely familiar with antioxidants as a marketable word printed on boxes of green tea or packets of dark chocolate, but apart from recognising vague claims such as that they help you live longer or stay healthier, many of us remain largely clueless about the actual benefits they provide. Gail knew antioxidants had cancer-fighting properties and the best place to find them were in fruits and vegetables, of which she already served plenty. But she set about finding more ways to load up Chris's diet with them and other supposedly beneficial foods for cancer treatment. He drank fresh fruit and vegetable juices, ate leafy salads, spinach, raw broccoli, beetroot, mushrooms, tomatoes and steamed vegetables. Homemade soups, omelettes and grilled fish were staples, with avocado, pawpaw, watermelon, goat's cheese, chickpeas and Manuka honey from New Zealand that was touted as having antibacterial and even regenerative qualities. Before dinner Dad usually enjoyed an appetiser of cheese and crackers, so Mum encouraged the alternative solution of crudités — raw vegetables like carrots and celery with hummus, taramasalata or other dips. She stewed apples to satisfy his sweet tooth. Blueberries (apparently the ultimate source of antioxidants) were scattered over his cereal and yoghurt or piled into a blender. Turmeric seemed to be a miracle spice with the potential to inhibit growth of new blood vessels in tumours. It was easily added to grilled fish or chicken.

One publication that landed on our doorstep described the Budwig protocol, the foundation of which is multiple daily servings of flaxseed oil and cottage cheese. I don't pretend to understand the scientific rationales behind this diet (or any of the regimes that Dad tried), but the Budwig diet appears to be based on a belief that cancer is linked to a lack of polyunsaturated fatty acids like omega-3, which is found in flaxseeds. Although its ability to treat cancer remains unproven, Gail was willing to add it into the mix and served Chris a delicious daily meal of bruschetta with tomatoes, basil and cottage cheese mixed with flaxseed oil.

Of course, some of the advice was contradictory. A naturopath insisted on a vegetarian diet but an immunobiologist later said red meat was crucial for a strong immune system. Many books and papers celebrated the humble almond as a super food that could fight cancer while others railed against foods with high levels of copper, which is found in almonds. Consistent 'no foods' were alcohol, caffeine and, most devastatingly, sugar. Dad did his best to cut it out of his diet but there was a paradox between doing whatever he could to survive and doing what he enjoyed in what were probably his final months of life. His sweet tooth defeated all comers, and my brothers and I were regular accomplices in trafficking contraband such as Mint Slices and Tim Tams into the house. One of my last text messages from him said, 'Hi darling, on your way home would you buy Paddle Pops or other ice-cream treats? XX.' On a couple of occasions, Guillaume brought Dad's absolute favourite: mini lemon tarts. I can still see Dad's eyes twinkle as he looked over his shoulder to make sure Mum wasn't looking before wolfing down his third.

Much later, Gail discovered the Canberra Medical Ecology Centre, where a clinical immunobiologist named Bill Giles offered holistic treatment with the goal of regenerating the immune system. Rather than using nutrition as a form of medicine, Mr Giles' methods were focused on the natural poisons, toxins and bugs in foods and testing how these burden a particular patient's immune system. There were some dietary changes to make as he recommended that Chris eat good-quality flesh foods — red meat, white meat and fish — cooked very well. In the following weeks Dad joked that he was now on a 'modified vegetarian' diet, which consisted of plenty of fresh fruit and vegetables ... plus meat. Off the menu, however, was grain produce. After meeting with Bill Giles, Chris's immune system was assessed as extremely vulnerable and in need of detoxing, and he was forbidden to eat grains: bread, pasta, biscuits, cakes, pastry or noodles. Grain-free pasta and bread that Mum bought from Deeks bakery in Canberra were stored in our pantry and freezer. Dad ate it uncomplainingly, although I mistook the bread for thick, bland cake. During the cleanse Dad also had to cut back on all that fresh fruit and legumes. Beer and wine were still out of the question.

Meanwhile, Gail was also dispensing dozens of supplements to which her research had led: Vitamins A, E and C, multivitamins, selenium, zinc, lysine, the list went on and on.

The benefits wrought by all of this are not easily evaluated. Perhaps the changes she made to his diet did make some difference and help him to live longer. But I believe that the greater benefit was that it offered my mother some kind of purpose and control. My father swallowed everything she handed him. Maybe he thought it could work, maybe he was simply willing to try anything that could help. But I suspect that he did it for her more than anything else.

My mother's and father's experience with cancer nutrition shaped strong views about the current state of nutritional advice for cancer patients. An unpalatable diet supplement and patchwork of research conducted by a desperate family member doesn't qualify as world-class treatment. Around this time, Chris delivered the Lambie Dew Oration at Sydney University in which he said that nutrition is 'one of the largest areas of deficiency' in conventional medical treatment. He went on: 'This sophisticated science uses intermittent weighing as almost the sole means of monitoring nutritional status and then facilitates maintenance or boosting of nutrition by providing chocolate- or banana-flavoured puke at a very reasonable cost to people who are totally anorexic or struggling with nausea and vomiting. We really have to do nutrition better. There is an enormous amount of information available about nutrition and cancer, quite apart from the advice to eat plenty of fresh fruit and vegetables, in books, publications and of course on the internet. Patients and their carers need to be industrious and energetic in seeking out this information because conventional sources of educational material are inadequate.'

The desperate search for a cure didn't just lead to tasteless bread and cottage cheese. Unconventional therapies found their unlikely way to my father by circuitous means. He was a man of science, the writer of more than a hundred scientific papers and seventeen book chapters during his career, and he created a database of head and neck cancers that became the largest in Australasia and one of the largest in the world. Yet desperation and a certain level of open-mindedness combined to take him to unexpected places.

Yin Yang Harmonisation Therapy was the creation of Leo Fang, a barrel-chested Mongolian-Chinese electrical therapist with a monk's haircut and thick staccato accent. He claimed that it would align the body's natural electrical frequencies and create better health — another goal of mind-numbing and immeasurable equivocality. For a few months in 2007, Chris attended sessions in this therapy twice a week, taking a ferry and then a bus to one of the clinics in Bondi Junction or Sydney's CBD. He would sit in a big leather armchair with his bare feet in a bucket of water and electrodes attached to his body's acupuncture pressure points. As electrical stimulation pulsed through his body, he would sit still and quietly, or chat with Mark Keighery, the man who had introduced him to the therapy.

Mark was fit and young and as the founder of the Marcs fashion label had been one of Australia's most successful fashion entrepreneurs when he was diagnosed with kidney cancer several years previously. He credited this daily treatment as being partly responsible for his good health and appetite in the face of disastrous metastases. Dad enjoyed talking with Mark, who was a family man as well as a successful businessman, and they shared moments of peace in the big comfortable chairs. These were the main reasons he went. But Leo became more persistent in his efforts to persuade Chris to help him promote his business. Eventually, this intruded a little too much upon the quiet of these afternoons and Chris stopped going.

A year later at the literary lunch for Chris's autobiography, *Never Say Die*, two people stationed themselves at the door of the Sofitel Wentworth's large dining room. The thin Chinese man smiled at me and bobbed his head as I took one of his small yellow flyers. 'Yin Yang Harmonisation Therapy', it trumpeted, listing everything it supposedly cured from asthma to sexual problems to cancer. I showed it to Dad, who asked Susan Wyndham, the *Sydney Morning Herald*'s literary editor and the master of ceremonies, to clarify to the room that he did not endorse it as a therapy.

It was a pity that Dad didn't feel comfortable going to Yin Yang because those moments essentially amounted to meditation for him. In general, he found it difficult to still his busy mind. Even at night, Mum would be kept awake by his toes wriggling in bed, a signal of the busyness behind his closed eyes. He was introduced to meditation by friends. Dr Tim Carr, who Chris knew from studying medicine, taught him Transcendental Meditation. A lean and quiet fellow with intense, deep-set eyes, Dr Carr would come to our home and try to teach the novice student. Chris was given his own secret mantra, and would work hard on meditating each day. But I would often find him sitting upright in an armchair with his head tilted back and mouth agape as he had fallen fast asleep within minutes. Another close friend recommended meditation sessions at a house in Crows Nest. But as Mum and Dad battled the peak-hour traffic to get there, managing the time and stress it took to attend another appointment, the meditation sessions seemed like a self-defeating exercise.

The *Sydney Morning Herald*'s *Good Weekend* magazine ran a story about Dad and afterwards we were flooded with letters and phone calls, many of which, again, contained advice and solutions. One call came from a man called Bill Sampson, a Nowra resident with white hair and a jolly laugh, who was spruiking a nutritional supplement called Immunocal in what seemed like a distribution channel similar to Amway cleaning products. Immunocal claims to boost glutathione levels in the body and, again, uses the rhetoric of antioxidants and immune function to explain its effect. It arrived in sachets of powder that were to be mixed with liquid. Dad winced as he drank the horrible white globular stuff. But, driven by desperation, Mum insisted he take it and would prepare the drink diligently, along with a sweet chaser to make it more bearable.

It's hard for me to hide my cynicism about these kinds of products. I don't know whether Immunocal works in some circumstances. Maybe it does. But I do know that any product that is expensive, foul-tasting and sold to dying people should have solid evidence that it works. Otherwise in my view, it is simply part of the big industry that markets to desperate families who have nothing to lose but money.

There were, of course, other alternative therapists whom my mother and father respected and trusted. A former trainee of my father's, Greg Lvoff, organised a magnificent evening at the harbour-front Aria restaurant as a kind of thank you and farewell from all my father's interns, registrars and overseas fellows over the years. Greg arranged for a limousine to carry the whole family there, showing sensitivity to the practical issues of driving and parking. The room hushed as Chris entered the restaurant; their tutor and mentor, whom they affectionately called 'Prof', now had unstable footing and pockmarked skin. During the evening Valerie Malka, a former intern who had since become head of trauma surgery at Westmead Children's Hospital, perched next to my parents and told them about her father, a homoeopath, naturopath and medical herbalist with expertise in cancers and chronic disease. She suggested they see him. Chris and Gail were immediately receptive, the suggestion coming as it did from a young surgeon with a serious medical background.

George Pierre Malka had kind eyes and a soft voice with a French accent. He had personally built up a compilation of anecdotal evidence of success in treating brain tumours using homoeopathy. Chris, who hadn't mentioned that he wasn't feeling well and had an upset stomach that day, sat down and George inspected his eyes.

'You've got a problem in your stomach,' George said.

'How did you know that?' Gail asked incredulously.

George showed Gail charts that delineated sections of the iris and how they related to corresponding organs. Although iridology derives patchy results in scientific studies, Gail's personal experience of witnessing this accurate diagnosis was persuasive.

George gave Chris an array of supplements (selenium, fish oil, echinacea, evening primrose oil, vitamin C and coenzyme Q10), a new diet (totally vegan, no alcohol, no sugar), a brown liquid made of herbal extracts and tiny homoeopathic tablets to be dissolved under the tongue. The 'black medicine', as it came to be called, was added to Chris's morning and afternoon swallowing schedule and was the most ghastly tasting thing he had had to take yet. But of all the alternative remedies they had tried, Chris and Gail felt most comfortable with this one.

They trusted George and while they knew that there were no guarantees, they placed some hope in his remedies.

Problems arose when the conventional and complementary treatments clashed. Dr Wheeler was an open-minded oncologist who understood that patients will search for answers wherever they think they can be found. 'We just don't know what the effect will be of taking that along with these chemotherapy drugs,' she warned. 'It is possible that they could decrease the efficacy of the drugs we're trying. We don't know how these things interact.' Meanwhile George Malka expressed his opinion that Chris should stop taking the chemotherapy so that his own treatment would have the opportunity to restore Chris's immune system and general wellbeing.

A routine MRI scan in December 2007 showed multiple white spots adjacent to the site of the original tumour. The biggest was eight millimetres across and at first this was interpreted as possible tumour regrowth. But doctors Wheeler and Teo believed they were actually changes in the tissue induced by the radiotherapy. Either way, Dr Wheeler suggested a pause from the chemo. Dad, always feeling somewhat nauseous and lethargic from it and with a depleted white blood cell count, welcomed the suggestion. George Malka was also pleased with the idea that Chris would continue on the supplements and homoeopathic alternatives without the interference of noxious medicines. Over the following months, the scans showed no progression of those white spots and in fact, they appeared to regress and to fade.

But it would not be long before a scan would reveal the relentless tumour on the march again, bringing my father to the crossroads of conventional medicine and less conventional treatments.

Some people have asked me why Chris — a doctor, a man of science — would try all of these unproven remedies. I believe the answer is that although he was a doctor, he was also a husband and a father. He tried them all for us.

Shedding the Ego

When Dad shaved his head, he bought a canvas hat with a narrow brim from a surf store. He often wore this or other hats to cover his bald head, and they had the effect of making him seem younger and smaller. He was wearing that hat one day as he and Mum walked from the RPA Medical Centre back to the car. Gail was holding his hand and leading him along, taking the small tentative steps that had become his new gait. She looked ahead, momentarily distracted, and didn't notice that she had stepped down a sloped gutter between the sidewalk and the road. Chris was unprepared for the drop when he stepped onto it. His ankle rolled over his foot and his body pulled on the ankle's tendon away from the joint. He collapsed with a cry as Gail gasped. She crouched down to him as he held the ankle between his hands, wincing as he rocked back and forth and she hugged him.

'I'm sorry, Christie, I'm sorry,' she said as the tears welled. 'I wasn't looking and—'

'It's okay, Pinkie, it's okay,' he consoled her, but his face showed the pain. Of all the moments I have asked my mother to describe, this is the one that upsets her more than any other. Chris was like a vulnerable child whom she felt she had allowed to be hurt. He was helpless and she was supposed to be his protector. It broke her heart to see him sitting in the street with yet more pain inflicted on him, wearing his little hat.

My mother was always gentle and tender in her care of my father. The long, angry gash in his scalp — the legacy of the three operations, radiotherapy and chemotherapy, which causes wound breakdown — was refusing to heal. He sat with his eyes closed as she dabbed cream onto the wound. She did up his buttons when his clumsy fingers couldn't manage. She was forever patient when his rebellious left hand caused a spill or a break. One time, when his and my attention was diverted by the TV, his left hand turned itself over and upturned an open tub of yoghurt, pouring the contents onto the couch.

My mother had originally struggled with this change in my father's identity. The sight of him sitting barefoot and bald-headed in those big armchairs doing Yin Yang Harmonisation Therapy caused her to bury her head in her hands. He seemed at peace with his fate, sitting in calmness and quiet. She clearly still had a way to go. But as 2008 wore on, Gail chaperoned and observed her changed husband during some remarkable moments.

He was invited to several overseas events by colleagues who wished to honour him and his contribution to the treatment of head and neck cancers. In May he received an award for excellence in surgery in Hong Kong, and in July Gail and Chris flew to San Francisco for the inaugural Chris O'Brien Lecture at the world head and neck conference. It was an enormous honour to have a lecture named after him, a mark of respect usually reserved for posthumous rewards. As my parents settled into their comfortable seats on the plane and clinked champagne glasses, it almost felt like old times again. But as the plane crossed the Pacific, Chris became more and more unwell. Isolated in his illness, he couldn't articulate to Gail what was wrong. Pounding headaches had returned and he felt nauseous most of the time. Gail worried they were symptoms of the cerebral oedema collecting again. American Express had been the only company willing to insure Dad to travel to the USA; what if he never got home?

In San Francisco they were upgraded to a suite, allowing Gail to sleep on the couch as Chris tossed and turned through the night. Somehow, he would pull on his suit as if it was armour and be sociable for the functions or lectures they had promised to attend. At a cocktail reception on San Francisco's waterfront, Gail kept Chris in her peripheral vision as she chatted with one of the other doctor's wives. It was a chilly evening but a lovely scene as the black-tie-clad fraternity drank wine by the city's wharves. The two women, who had met regularly over the years, chatted as friends, but when the woman made her goodbyes, she said, 'Well, it's been nice knowing you,' leaving Gail to contemplate the only meaning this comment could have.

They stopped in Hawaii on the return journey and Gail wandered around Waikiki Beach on her own when Chris was too sick to come out. She came upon a small tipi tent with an Irish fortune teller inside. *No, it's silly*, she thought and went to walk away. But the Irish female voice called out to her, and she thought, *What's the harm?* and stepped into the kitsch little marquee. 'There's something that you don't think you're any good at. But you are,' the woman said. She went on with more platitudes, but didn't say what Gail wanted to hear — that he's going to be fine.

In September they travelled again, this time to England for Chris to deliver the prestigious Semon Lecture at the Royal Society of Medicine, London. He spoke on skin cancer of the head and neck and received a rapturous standing ovation. But while his peers paid him more respect than ever, his illness mandated perspective. 'Makes you wonder if they need a little more excitement in their lives,' he joked with Gail back in their hotel room.

Back in Sydney, Gail drove Chris to an increasing number of speaking engagements, from community events to large soirees. Rather than seeing his illness as a reason to retreat from the world, it pushed him further into it. His illness brought him closer to people and gave him a bigger platform. 'I feel like I'm the owner of a celebrity brain tumour,' he used to jest. 'I feel like saying to this thing, this is all your fault, why don't you go and talk to these people, how come I've gotta do the talking?'

Gail watched how people approached Chris — strangers who had watched him on RPA and were now following his story in the newspapers and on television. They would tell him about their own journeys and hug him like a brother. It was obvious that while my father had always been driven by an altruistic calling, his experiences were revealing a new level of compassion and empathy.

He attended mass more regularly, giving generously to the collection plates. He could not walk through the city without stopping for each homeless man or woman who sat in our path, often giving a ten- or twenty-dollar note or offering to buy them lunch. On one occasion, I stood back as he crouched down to a man sitting with his dog in a busy shopping area. The two chatted for a minute, before Dad stood up and walked back to me, smiling. 'He's vegetarian.' He eyed a Japanese restaurant behind us. 'Wait here, I'll get him some sushi.'

He was asked to speak at his old high school, Parramatta Marist Brothers, where he told the boys that men of steel have compassion in their hearts. He urged the Australian Medical Students' Association meeting in Melbourne to treat patients as though they were members of their own families. He confessed that his own diagnosis and treatment had changed him as a doctor, giving him a more holistic understanding of the patient experience.

Gail had told her obstetrician years before that she wasn't the woman she had been. 'Better,' he had responded. So it was with my mother and father now. They weren't the woman and man they had been when my father's illness began; they were better. By the year's end, stopped at traffic lights, Gail turned to her husband. 'You know, it's been such a terrible year,' she said. 'But I wouldn't have been without it.'

After a few seconds of silence, he responded, 'Neither would I.'

My dear mother,

You said to me recently, 'It's not really a life worth living if there's no suffering.' Do you really believe that?

Love Juliette

* * *

My darling,

You and I have both heard people use ridiculous platitudes like, 'Haven't you got over it?'

Why is it brought into your life in the first place if all you do is 'get over it'?

You don't get over things. You keep them with you and learn from them. You live by them. It doesn't bury you but you live with it. What is the point in life if you don't learn from it?

Your father learned so much during this time. He grew more through his own illness than through twenty years of medicine.

Love Mum

The Tumour, a Gift

Chris's determination to establish Australia's first comprehensive cancer centre quickened as his life shortened. The million dollars from the NSW Iemma government had produced a sustainable business case based on a not-for-profit model. Within days of his diagnosis Chris recognised the tumour as a weapon in his advocacy arsenal; his prominence as a cancer surgeon and the lethal nature of his disease combined to give him unequalled authority to speak on cancer care in Australia. He used the tumour as a means of placing the question of Australia's model of cancer treatment on the national agenda, writing an opinion piece in the *Sydney Morning Herald* in which he laid out the case for a move away from the 150-year-old public teaching hospital model to comprehensive cancer centres. New South Wales, he wrote, should have 'at least one world-class cancer centre where diagnosis, cutting-edge treatment, caring cancer support, high-quality research and a fertile academic environment are integrated to facilitate ground-breaking discoveries, the development of new and innovative therapies and the achievement of better treatment outcomes'.

But Chris's solicitations for support from the federal minister for health Tony Abbott were meeting a 'comprehension gap', in Chris's words. ABC radio announcer Adam Spencer on several occasions interviewed Chris on his high-profile and popular program. Listening to the interviews today, it occurs to me that Dad spoke like a man with nothing to lose, saying that Abbott was in denial of the need for a research centre of excellence.

'My suggestion to [Tony Abbott] was that the federal government's got money sort of literally falling out of its pocket, and holy mackerel, for the cost of a submarine or an F-18 or whatever jet plane they're gonna buy next, they could build two or three of these cancer centres. And if the federal government grasped the nettle and said, "Okay, we'll agree that there should be a national network of world-class comprehensive cancer centres, and we'll contribute infrastructure funding to those, and help them to become centres of research excellence where research is integrated with the clinical care", then I think that'd be a big contribution. But Mr Abbott doesn't get that.'

In an interview the following week, Abbott responded, 'I have tremendous respect for Chris O'Brien professionally, and obviously I very much appreciate the difficult personal situation he's in, and there's a sense in which Chris O'Brien has tremendous moral standing on this issue and I guess as a health minister I'm a bit overawed by that ... But we have a professional body we have recently established called Cancer Australia to advise us, and I think it would be fair to say that so far Cancer Australia is not convinced that establishing a small number of so-called integrated cancer centres is necessarily the way to go.'

So with a federal election looming in late 2007, Chris turned his attention to the Opposition and met with the Labor leader Kevin Rudd. A Queenslander, former diplomat and not one to be tapped into the minor celebrity status bestowed on people by reality TV, Mr Rudd had had no idea who Chris was. Yet during a one-hour meeting at Sydney's Radisson hotel while Rudd was on the campaign trail, Chris convinced Kevin Rudd of the value of this policy. About a month before the election, the Labor leader pledged $50 million for a new purpose-built cancer centre on the RPA campus.

Labor was elected to government and on the same historic day that the prime minister apologised to the Stolen Generations, 13 February 2008, my mother drove my father to the nation's capital to meet with him. Gail wasn't to know then that in seven years to the day she would be standing on the podium at the Chris O'Brien Lifehouse, and in front of prime minister Tony Abbott, former prime minister Kevin Rudd and a host of other dignitaries, she'd be speaking at the opening of the operating theatres and inpatients wards.

On the day he met with prime minister Kevin Rudd, my father had lost all vision on his left side and could become easily confused and disoriented. Gail held his hand as they walked from the car into Parliament House. She even pointed him towards the correct doorway when the prime minister's aide called Chris in. But while the location of the tumour had affected Chris's sight, balance and coordination, it had left intact the qualities he needed to push for his cause: a quick mind, compelling use of speech and convincing personality.

Gail waited for Chris outside the prime minister's office. When the two men emerged, she saw them interact in what was clearly the beginnings of a friendship. Over the following months, they would exchange text messages more and more frequently in a comradeship forged on similar backgrounds, shared beliefs and deep, reciprocal respect.

Beyond comprehensive cancer care, Chris was increasingly speaking about holistic treatment. His and Gail's journey, traversing the myriad specialists, treatments, and complementary and alternative therapies, had given them new insight into the fragmented paths NSW cancer patients are forced to tread.

The monthly MRI scans kept coming around. We enjoyed an entire year without another operation and the scans had shown during that time that Dad's brain was free of cancer. But in the middle of 2008, the images showed unmistakable progression of the tumour. The date for a fourth operation was set down for June.

'Don't do it, Chris,' George Malka said. 'Don't have the surgery.' For the previous year George had been dispensing homoeopathic remedies which my mother and father compliantly took. Chris's general wellness and immunity had improved since he took a break from the chemo. George believed that surgery would set this course back. But as much as my father respected George, he could not shun surgery in favour of unproven remedies.

The anxiety we had all felt leading up to the previous surgeries had given way to resignation. My mother knew that once she left Dad in the hands of Charlie Teo, there was nothing she could do. She had complete faith in Charlie, and her job was to get Dad to the hospital, as it was to get him to the airport for a flight. Charlie focused on debulking the main mass of the tumour and the procedure didn't cause Chris any further problems. In fact, he felt so well that from his hospital bed he complained to me that he wanted to lose a couple of kilos around his belly and asked me to take him for a walk around the block.

As planned, this fourth operation bought us more time. We did not know then, though, how little.

In October 2008, Mr Rudd launched Chris's memoir, *Never Say Die*. Chris had been approached by HarperCollins to write the book and he'd dictated it in the space of a few months. At its launch, Chris told the room that, just three months after his fourth operation, the latest scan had revealed two nodules of tumour adjacent to the main mass. True to the defining features of glioblastoma multiforme, the tumour's tentacles had fanned out through his brain, and nodules, like new small tumours, were materialising in new places in the cancer's web.

As Dad was facing a month-long publicity tour and countless television and radio interviews for his book, Dr Wheeler put him on a new course of chemotherapy drugs by infusion. You might ask why Chris and Gail would say yes to a book publicity road show when he was so unwell. But the reason is simple — it was an adventure. He was not thinking about impending death; he was still thinking about what life remained. Precious life! It was so unexpected to have new experiences that were fun at this point. Besides that, each talk or interview was another opportunity for him to state his case for comprehensive cancer care.

One morning near dawn as Gail drove Chris to a breakfast television program, she said he looked too rundown. 'You're taking on too many things, Christie. You need to say "no" occasionally.'

'But talking about myself is one of the only things I'm still good for,' he said, smiling.

A few days after his fifty-seventh birthday, Chris pulled himself out of bed mid-morning. He was scheduled to give an interview to the ABC a couple of hours later, but he was not feeling well. His head was pulsing and his mouth was bone-dry. Gail went through the usual motions. She brought him his medications, prepared some breakfast and helped him get dressed.

She drove him to the ABC studios in Ultimo, as he rested his head on his hand. As she parked she told him they were running late, and rushed around to help him out of the car. Chris could not move any faster. He heaved himself out and took Gail's hand. They started walking extremely slowly. Gail knew that this pace was ominous. Each time the oedema collected in his head, his steps would become slower, deliberate yet uncertain.

Small step by small step, they made their way to the studio. Chris greeted the team and sat in the chair with the microphone before him. Then he began to talk and his voice sounded strong, deep and composed.

'How are you feeling?' ABC presenter Michael Peschardt asked live on air.

'I feel well,' Chris said with lightness in his voice. 'Mornings are not my best time, even though this is late morning, this is about my getting up on time.' And he laughed. 'But apart from that I'm well.'

Gail stood with the producers in the studio's antechamber, watching and listening through the glass. She shook her head, not in disapproval, but disbelief at his composure. No one listening to the radio could possibly hear what she could see.

As the interview continued, Michael asked Chris whether there were times when he was angry. 'No. In the last couple of weeks, it's interesting and I don't know why this is — I'm due to have a scan tomorrow — I have thought of death a little more. I'm still not frightened of dying. Death doesn't really frighten me.'

'Why not?'

'I don't know why. But I'm just not frightened of having that final sleep. I don't think there's anything to fear. What can happen to you? I'm not in pain. When my death comes I won't be in pain. It concerns me in relation to my three children and my wife, who I think will find it very, very difficult ... Sitting there and wondering how they'll cope and what their future lives will be like is concerning and perhaps it's something better not done. You can tie yourself in knots wondering about what will happen to one's children or one's wife and how their lives will play out. But I have no control over that.'

'The public response to you — how much of a comfort has that been?'

'Oh, it's been extraordinary. Even at the time of my diagnosis, I was just flooded with so much warmth and concern and support and love, from all over ... the sentiments with which [people] expressed their feelings were just extraordinarily kind and generous. They were just so nice to me.'

'It's a terrible way to realise that, isn't it?'

'Well, I suppose it is, but apart from the fact that I'll probably die from this illness — apart from that — it's really been an extraordinary gift and this journey has been really remarkable.'

'See, I'm blown away by the way you can say that with, I don't know, equanimity? I don't know. But with so much objectivity, and calm grace and courage. Where does that come from?'

'I don't know, to be honest. As I said, I'm not fearful of dying. And I think this thing will catch up with me. I hope it's later rather than sooner.' He had taught us how to live. Now he was teaching us how to die.

The next day Chris had the scan and spoke to Charlie on the phone. Charlie was frank. 'You'll be dead in a month if you don't have an operation,' he said. There was significant progression of one of the nodules — now measuring four centimetres — and a lot of swelling of the brain. They scheduled another brain operation — Chris's fifth — for the following day. From that surgery, my father would never recover.

Witness to Grace

The operation on 9 January 2009 lasted five hours. It took an hour and a half for the surgical team to pull and stitch the large wound in his scalp closed. When Chris awoke, he murmured, 'No more. No more.'

'All right, Christie, no more,' Gail whispered into his ear and kissed his cheeks and forehead.

A day later Chris developed a dense left-sided paralysis that left him unable to move that side of his body at all. Thankfully, it resolved as quickly as it had appeared. He came home four days later with that long gash more painful than ever. A hole the size of a pinprick opened up at its centre. The skin was refusing to remain sealed and heal. Dad started carrying a bottle of antibiotics around his neck or in a bumbag, flowing through a PICC [Peripherally Inserted Central Catheter] line into his left arm to prevent infection of the wound.

The rollercoaster was relentless and we took each high, dip and swerve at a time. A high, such as spending a few days at a friend's splendid apartment in Surfers Paradise, enjoying family barbecues and wading in the rooftop pool, was inevitably followed by a low, with the flight home punctuated by a night in hospital as brain swelling caused Chris to suffer double vision, vomiting, a bad headache and confusion.

The dense paralysis returned and his left side weakened further. Soon he could not walk without the aid of a walking stick. As Dad tapped his way down the hall or jokingly drummed it at his feet like Ebenezer Scrooge, the borrowed cane from the chemist made a distinctive sound — more a chink than a thud — that I can still hear. The paralysis waxed and waned, but overall he needed more and more physical help. James spent a lot of time helping our father in practical ways such as getting up and down the stairs and dressing in the morning. Dad fell on a couple of occasions while trying to get into bed and James would be there to help Mum lift him up. 'Jamesie boy, you'll have the perfect excuse if you ever become a serial killer, having to help your naked father off the floor,' Dad said.

The pinpoint hole in the wound grew, splitting the skin apart more and more. It revealed a dark crevasse into his skull, as a clear fluid — the cerebral oedema — oozed out. He asked me to take a photo of the wound so that he could inspect from the photo whether it was infected. It was not, and in fact we were later told probably prolonged his life for several more months because it drained the fluid away and relieved the intensifying pressure in his head. The leaking wound required daily dressing, which my mother did, as well as gentle community nurses who came to the house.

As the pressure mounted in the right side of Chris's brain, the left side of his face began to droop and his speech became slurred. But he used all this to full effect when joke-telling. Whether he was impersonating a deranged lion tamer, a bartender with a speech impediment or a woman with a deaf schnauzer, he wove evermore absurd stories with bizarre characters and voices. 'They're your jokes now,' he told my mother's brother and sister-in-law, Murray and Lyndall, after lunch one day.

I don't recall seeing my mother cry as her strong, robust husband deteriorated before her eyes. She cared for his every need with determination and a singularity of purpose.

Her desperate search for life-saving formulae continued to close to the end. The last thing she tried was a plant extract called methyl jasmonate which she imported from the USA. Even though it was unlisted on the Pharmaceutical Benefits Scheme and regarded as a complete wild card by the medical establishment, Dr Wheeler had supported Gail to help her source it from overseas. Chris obligingly took the methyl jasmonate, drawing it through his airways from a diffuser of hot water. But it started to make his nose bleed, on top of everything else, and she knew that her attempts to save him had to end.

For all my mother's work — her searching, researching, cooking, experimenting and driving — no matter what she did, Chris never got better. This was not like the flu or a viral illness that comes and goes. It wasn't like the tonsillitis he'd had when they were in Paris all those years before. It was always there. 'I would cut off my right arm if it would make you better, Christie,' Gail said. But nothing could make him better.

One day, she went out for a walk on her own and a word occurred to her repeatedly: accept. She had to accept. She had reached that point.

On Good Friday Adam, James and I attended mass with our father. The afternoon service was a sombre one, marking Jesus Christ's crucifixion. Villa Maria's tabernacle was stripped of its ornaments and the altar lay bare. Father Kevin and assisting clergy entered in silence without the usual singing, and the solemn liturgy began. A large crucifix was unveiled and held up at the front of the church. One by one, people stepped forward to venerate the cross by kissing or touching the wood or Christ's feet. My father began to rise and my brothers held out their arms to support him. Dad took their hands and the three of them edged out of the pew and inched together down the aisle. He leaned on his sons as he knelt to the ground and kissed Christ's feet. I saw our parish friends wipe away tears.

When it came time for communion, I approached Father Kevin alone. The afternoon sun streamed through a stained-glass window behind me. As he held out the wafer, Father Kev's head tilted up, and his glasses and wet eyes caught the light, reflecting it back to me. He squeezed my hand as he placed the wafer within.

Around this time, Dad wrote to my brothers and me.

My darlings,

What do you value? What are your values? What principles guide your planning and actions and then allow you to examine and judge those actions?

Try to have a think.

The following, I think, are worth keeping in your hearts:

1. *Tolerance*

2. *Fairness*

3. *Kindness*

4. *Honesty (absolute, including with yourself)*

5. *Hard work — remember EQ (effort quotient) overrides IQ*

6. *Loyalty–faithfulness.*

7. *I adore you all,*

8.

9. *1 and 2*

10. *Recognise the rights of others*

Working hard to live by your principles takes effort, conviction and frequent review.

This note captures my dad in so many ways, not just what he was like as a father and mentor, or what his own values were, but his knack for inserting the unexpected, like the way he left number eight blank and used number nine to make us look again at points one and two.

Dad's advocacy work continued with more urgency than ever. I would often find him in the study typing emails with just the index finger on his right hand as his left arm hung heavily, almost lifelessly, down his side. Since securing funding from the federal government, plans for a comprehensive cancer centre at Royal Prince Alfred Hospital, to be called Lifehouse at RPA, progressed rapidly. Chris continued to make phone calls and send emails at all hours of the day and night. These things consumed his time and energy as he attempted to lay the foundations for a successful centre by putting in place a strong board of directors and executive team.

Lifehouse at RPA was launched on 17 April 2009 at a reception at NSW Government House, where the prime minister Kevin Rudd announced further funding of $100 million. Adam helped Dad to the stage and stood protectively behind him, like a sentinel, for the duration of his speech. As newspaper photographers clamoured around them afterwards, Kevin Rudd and Chris sat chatting on the balcony. Mr Rudd held Chris's saucer so that he could use his working hand to raise a teacup to his lips.

Kevin Rudd suggested that he attend mass with us the following Sunday. He came with his teenage curly-headed son Marcus, and sat in the pew next to Dad. During communion

Mr Rudd said, 'I brought a present for you, mate,' and pulled a small red box out of his pocket. It contained black rosary beads given to him by Pope Benedict. As Dad accepted this precious and generous gift, he was overcome by emotion, and briefly and quietly wept. Afterwards Kevin and Marcus came to our home for afternoon tea and chatted easily with the family and parishioners who joined us. Other than polite Australian Federal Police officers checking out the house before his arrival, and Guillaume bringing trays full of exquisite finger food, it felt like any other autumn afternoon tea that Chris had hosted.

By now scans were showing a large amount of tumour progression and the right hemisphere of Chris's brain was overwhelmed with swelling. The tumour was also edging into his brain's left hemisphere, his dominant side. Dad now needed constant care. His left side became progressively paralysed and when his left leg stopped responding we arranged for a wheelchair in the house. Mum and Dad moved into my bedroom, which was downstairs. James maintained the responsibilities of undressing him at night and helping him into bed. I read to him and typed his dictations. Adam spent the afternoons in his company. His pleasures were simple — he listened to music, satisfied his sweet tooth, drank a little pinot noir and continued to read and be read to. Each morning Mum would shower him, dress him and brush his hair. He sat in his wheelchair, looking into the mirror, as she gently smoothed his hair away from his face.

'How do I look?' he asked.

'Dr Gorgeous,' she replied.

Most evenings, he would ask one of us to help him to the cellar to pick a bottle of pinot gris. Gail loved the sweet white wine and Chris loved choosing it for her. It was a simple but thoughtful thing that he could still do.

There were some awful moments. Perhaps our worst night was when we forgot to turn off his electric blanket as we put him to bed. He awoke to find himself baking but was too paralysed to move. He called out to us repeatedly. We were just on the other side of the wall, but the television was turned up too loudly. When someone finally heard his weak cries, the bed was soaked and he was beside himself.

But there were beautiful moments too. Once I was helping Dad move from his wheelchair to an armchair. While he was still seated, he tried kicking something out of the way with his working leg, and somehow his whole body slipped in one quick movement so he was half hanging off the chair, his back parallel to the floor. I quickly wrapped my arms around his thighs to keep him from falling and as I hugged him and we ineffectively struggled to heave him up, we broke into laughter, which became more of a hindrance than his paralysis. We had to call Mum and James, who were more expert at the heavy-lifting duties than I was.

His spirit would always bounce back. 'We will hold our heads high and not be defeated by this,' he told Mum.

On Monday 1 June 2009, Dad and Mum enjoyed a beautiful night at the luxurious Katoomba resort Lilianfels, a gift from Adam, James and me for Mother's Day. They ate high tea and admired the lovely rooms with toile wallpaper, accompanied by James and his girlfriend, Lulu, and their old dear friends Susie and Lawrie Hayden. Chris was very infirm by this stage and hugely reliant on James and Lawrie to transfer him from his wheelchair into the car or bed. On the drive home, he said to Gail, 'I feel like I'm hanging from a thread; that you're all hanging from the same thread. And that I should cut you free.'

Back at home, winter was setting in with grey skies and cold rain. Dad sat by the window in the sitting room.

'Christie,' Mum said. 'We need to talk about your service.'

'Yes, all right.' Dad had turned his mind to his own funeral soon after first being diagnosed, but had capped the mental energy it required while he focused on living. Now, Gail sat with a pen and paper and jotted down some notes of eulogists, music and other details. Together, it was like they were planning another fundraising function. When they finished, he said, 'It's going to be good. I'd like to be there.'

He held the rosary beads that Kevin Rudd had given to him. He had taught Gail the comforting rhythm of the prayer with which he had grown up and through which he now found solace.

Hail Mary, full of grace,
The Lord is with thee,
Blessed art thou amongst women,
And blessed is the fruit of thy womb Jesus,
Holy Mary, mother of God, pray for us now,
And at the hour of our death.
Amen

My darling,

Your father's was a very public dying. Chris, the inspirational surgeon's surgeon, became the teacher of how to die with grace and dignity. I was simply a privileged observer. There was no pulling back from this.

I am humbled and motivated by the memory of his suffering.

Rendered incapacitated, paralysed and blinded at times as his health deteriorated, he continued unabated in his quest until his very last day. Not for himself, he had nothing to gain. His response to this grave adversity was honourable and inspirational. The image of him thwarted at every turn by his failing health was nothing short of sacramental.

He had been stripped of everything we continue to hold onto. The constraints of ego, the bondage of self-absorption, the politics of power and all that remained were the purest of motives.

Love, Mum

The End

It began with a sudden and most acute headache in the early afternoon of Wednesday 3 June 2009.

Appointments in the Order of Australia had been released to media ahead of the announcements on the Queen's Birthday public holiday. Chris had been appointed an Officer of the Order and I had spent the morning fielding calls for interviews. From the moment he had woken up, Dad had been quiet. Mum made him scrambled eggs and he ate them slowly. Nursing staff came to change his wound dressing and he didn't make his usual friendly quips. A journalist and a photographer from the *Sydney Morning Herald* came. I escorted them into the lounge room where Dad had spent so much time over the previous two and a half years. I kissed him goodbye and left for a seminar at university. Outside, the day was grey and overcast with a spattering of rain. Dark silver light filtered in through the window.

When he was alone again, sitting in his blue armchair and nursing a slight headache that did not seem particularly unusual, it is more than likely that the tumour ruptured a blood vessel and caused a bleed in his brain. He called to Gail softly, a sound as loud as he could muster. The pain inside his skull quickly became so excruciating that he could barely speak beyond a whisper. Gail heard him and ran in. The cerebral spinal fluid was leaking out of the hole in his head. She rang Dr Wheeler, who told her to bring him into the hospital for a scan.

'Christie,' Mum whispered as Chris held his head down with his eyes closed. 'Helen said to come in for a scan.'

'There's no point,' he said. 'I'm dying. I need some morphine.'

She knew it too.

The plan had been for Dad to die at home. The previous day a bed had been delivered from Greenwich Hospital palliative care unit and set up in my bedroom. But in fact we were completely unprepared for him to die at home for one main reason — there was no morphine in the house.

Gail phoned the local medical centre and asked for Chris's GP. The receptionist told her that he was having eye surgery, and Gail asked for somebody to come quickly.

She hung up and waited next to Chris. When nobody arrived she phoned again. But the doctor who was on duty said she had a waiting room full of patients, and could not get there.

'Don't let me die in pain,' Chris said. And Gail knew she was letting him down. She had to get some morphine. She dialled Triple 0. The operator told her to 'get the patient lying down'. Gail didn't want instructions. She just wanted them to bring morphine. She was on the phone a few minutes later when the doorknocker slammed. Our dog barked. 'Can you get that dog and put it in another room?' asked the operator.

Two young paramedics stood on the doorstep.

'Thank God. My husband needs morphine.'

'We don't have any morphine,' they said. 'We'll need to call an ICU ambulance for that.'

Gail was on the verge of tears. One of the paramedics called for an ICU ambulance and ran up the driveway to wait for it. The other, a young woman, waited with Mum. Helpless, they crouched by Chris, who barely moved or acknowledged they were there. Finally a third paramedic arrived from the ICU ambulance. He said he had no intention of administering any morphine unless Gail said Chris was going to hospital. 'But he wants to be at home!' Gail said. 'We've got the palliative equipment for him to die at home.'

They carried him to the hospital bed. But still the paramedic refused to administer the morphine unless Gail agreed to take him to hospital. When she did, he gave it to Chris immediately. As the morphine seeped into his veins and started to do its work, the skies opened up and it started to pour. Dad was bundled onto a stretcher and the straps were fastened around him. The ambulance sat at the top of our steep driveway and Mum and James held umbrellas over his body while the paramedics pushed him up the hill. The ambulance doors swung open and Chris was slid inside.

The cruel irony of it all, Gail thought. *His own death such a mess, and after he has done so much.*

'Mum, can I go with Dad?' James asked.

'Okay, I'll get his things and see you at the hospital.'

About ten minutes into the journey to the hospital, Dad looked up at James and murmured, 'Where's Mum?'

'She's coming behind us,' James said. He gave a tiny nod as he acknowledged the answer. Then he lost consciousness.

Adam and I were called and the family congregated in Gloucester House, where one of Dad's colleagues led us into a small room. We sat in soft chairs and listened to oncologist Dr Lisa Horvath telling us there was nothing they could do. Mum stood up and walked out to Dad, who was lying asleep on a bed nearby. She held his hand and called in his right ear. 'Christie!' He opened his eyes, turned his head and looked at her. They locked eyes and he smiled at her for the last time.

He was moved to a room on level 10 of RPA that overlooked the University of Sydney campus. We kept vigil for the next thirty hours as his big, strong heart continued to pump life through his body. Extended family, friends and colleagues moved gently in and out. His breathing became laboured and at about four in the morning he suddenly sat bolt upright. 'Dad!' we said, hoping for a miracle yet. But his green eyes looked at us without recognition. He spewed vomit and we yelled to each other to roll him on his side. We squeezed his cheeks and tried to unclench his jaw as he groaned. And then he was gone again, into the depths of unconsciousness.

As Dad lay in that hospital bed, his body restless and sometimes letting out a long, deep groan, a powerful passage from Joseph Conrad's novel *Heart of Darkness* echoed in my head:

> *I have wrestled with death. It is the most unexciting contest you can imagine. It takes place in an impalpable greyness, with nothing under foot, without spectators, without glory, without the great desire for victory, without a fear of defeat, in a sickly atmosphere of tepid scepticism, without much belief in your own rights and even less in those of your adversary.*

As the hours passed, his body eased into greater and greater gentleness. Mum tried to remove his wedding ring, but it hadn't been removed for months and was now stuck so tightly over his swollen finger that it wouldn't budge. A nurse brought in metal cutters and clamped down on the handles with all her force to break the ring free. My mother fingered the ring and put it in her pocket.

At about six in the evening, Kevin Rudd arrived, having flown to Sydney straight after parliament to be here. He gave each of us a big squeeze. 'My God, you've been a brick,' he said to Mum. Then he stood by Chris's bedside, held his hand and read the citation for his Order of Australia. 'Whereas with the approval of Her Majesty Queen Elizabeth the Second, Queen of Australia and Sovereign of the Order of Australia, I have been pleased to appoint you to be an Officer in the General Division of the Order of Australia.' Respecting the sanctity of the circumstance, he stayed just a few minutes more.

The last two hours of my father's life were peaceful. His breathing became lighter and lighter. As it did, a dense white fog settled on inner Sydney. It curled through the streets and engulfed the football fields and sandstone buildings of the University of Sydney that I could see from the window of that hospital room.

Shallower and shallower, his breath became still. Was he still drawing air? It was hard to tell. I lay my head on the soft, white sheet next to his body and watched for the tiniest movement in his chest. There could be a miracle yet, I prayed. But then he didn't breathe again. It was just after eight o'clock at night on Thursday 4 June. Outside the fog hovered close to the earth. Nothing moved. Nothing changed. There was no cataclysmic crash of thunder or howling from the skies. The world simply continued to spin. And we were left standing on it.

PART THREE

Till Death Do Us Part

Afterlife

We could not leave his body. We stayed and stroked his hair and rested our hands on his skin. We cut locks of his hair, and James took the hospital band from around his wrist. His muscles were still warm and soft. He looked peaceful and like himself. It was impossible to believe that life had simply lifted out of his body. His face became slightly more pale. The skin on his back turned a deep purple as the blood coagulated. After about an hour, Mum pulled Adam, James and me away, saying that we would be able to see Dad again before the funeral. We limped to the car, which floated home through the fog still engulfing the streets that we knew so well. At home, I went upstairs to Mum's room and as I turned the corner, she slumped to the floor in tears. 'Oh, Mum,' I said, hugging her.

I woke the next morning at seven to the sounds of the television in the next room. Listening from my pillow, I heard the presenters of a breakfast television show talking about Dad.

I turned my eyes from the ceiling to the bedside table. His glasses sat there. Nearby, the red cashmere jumper that he'd been wearing on his last morning at home hung over a chair. I put the jumper on and went out to the living room. My uncle Phil and aunt Carmel were staying with us, as they would for a few weeks. Phil, always the earliest riser, was standing by the gas fireplace, watching the TV.

'Morning, Jet,' he said. 'How'd you sleep? Have a look at the paper.' He motioned towards the kitchen. I walked over and picked up the *Herald*. A sad photo of Dad was on the front page. He looked puffy, disabled, wrecked. He made no pretences for the picture. It was taken two days earlier for the story about the Queen's Birthday Honours. He wore the same jumper that I was wearing now. *But he was just here*, I thought. I couldn't fathom that he wasn't here now. His walking stick still leaned against the blue armchair where he had sat that morning. The book he had been reading still had its bookmark in place. How could he not exist any more?

On the TV, a news presenter animatedly talked about the irony of Chris dying from the same disease that he cured for many other people — a neat narrative, but not entirely accurate. (Chris operated on the soft tissues of the head and neck; not the brain.) As the morning talk about Dad continued, Phil turned to me, mystified. 'When did this happen?' I knew what he meant. When did Dad become so high profile? I turned my palms upwards. 'I don't know.'

I went back to bed and awoke later to the sounds of a full house buzzing from behind my door. The smell of flowers — oriental lilies, gardenias and roses — swept me up as I crept towards the study. There, I found Mum hanging up the phone. She looked well. Fresh from a few hours sleep and in organising mode, she was calm and measured.

'Darling, the corneal transplant unit called,' she said. 'Dad elected to be a donor. They were calling for permission to transplant his cornea.'

'Really?'

'I told them yes. Is that all right?'

'Of course.'

'Also, Kevin Rudd telephoned. He asked if I'd accept a state funeral for Dad. Of course I said yes.'

'Wow.' I was taken aback. She didn't appear to be.

It is a prerogative of the prime minister of the day to order a state funeral. My father's was the only state funeral that Kevin Rudd ever ordered. As many people know, organising a funeral is a big deal under ordinary circumstances. You are essentially holding a large function with logistical peculiarities, which might be attended by everyone you know, and you have about a week to prepare. But agreeing to a state funeral introduced many issues we'd never considered. The Department of Prime Minister and Cabinet was now involved, as were the NSW government, state police, federal police and St Mary's Cathedral, where the requiem mass would be held.

There were questions of protocol, governmental requirements and discussions about who paid for what. There was the writing and approval of state funeral announcements, whether the national anthem would be sung and the Australian flag draped over the casket. Lifehouse material, ushers and seating arrangements in the cathedral had to be arranged. There was even, I later learned, a request for the micro-management of places in the pews for certain dignitaries who did not want to be seen by or sat next to one another.

All these issues were fielded and dealt with by Paul Cave. Paul was one of Dad's former patients who had become a great friend and something of a mentor. A businessman and entrepreneur who founded Sydney's BridgeClimb, Paul has been a director of the Chris O'Brien Lifehouse for years. He had been my father's confidant during long chats into the night at Paul's offices near the southern pylon of the Harbour Bridge. I understand that they talked about Chris's worries, his regrets, his triumphs — and Paul gave Chris assurances of being there for Gail after his death. Paul began to fulfil his word immediately, stepping in as the family representative in all matters relating to the state funeral.

A series of meetings were held at our home and a few days before the funeral was scheduled to take place, a meeting at St Mary's cathedral house brought all the parties together. Adam and I chose to accompany Mum. I stepped out of the car, my shoulders so heavy I thought I might have to sit on the pavement.

But then my big brother gave me one of his quintessential bear hugs. Adam was solid as a statue as we stood in the shadow of the cathedral, his thick, hairy arms wrapped around me.

Inside the cathedral house, tables had been arranged in a large circle and close to twenty people were already seated or standing nearby. Some of the faces I recognised and I was particularly thankful for the familiar face of Father Kevin, our parish priest and family friend who would conduct the service. Paul Cave gave us long, warm hugs, as did another dear friend of the family, Keith Cox, who would also play a large role in the planning of the service. A leading nurse and head of the oncology chemotherapy unit at RPA, Keith had brought whatever we needed to the home as Dad became more unwell. Now he would be the acolyte (or assistant) during the requiem mass, continuing to perform a guardian angel role for our family. Patsy Healy and John Harris, the gentle and kind representatives from W.N. Bull Funerals, were there. The assistant secretary of the ceremonial and hospitality branch of the Department of Prime Minister and Cabinet attended with two colleagues. There were also representatives from the NSW Department of Premier and Cabinet, COMCAR, NSW Police, a communications firm and Lifehouse at RPA, as it was then known. Dev Gopalasamy from the performing arts department of Riverview was coordinating the music. Father Paul Hilder, the dean of St Mary's Cathedral, and Mari Palomares, the event coordinator, were there.

Mum, Adam and I took our seats. Paul opened the meeting, inviting everyone to introduce themselves, and, in his calm and measured way, outlined the details needing agreement and points of logistical challenge. As he spoke, with his tall frame leaning back and long fingers motioning through the air, it was obvious that he had a preternatural ability to consider and foresee the most intricate details. The discussion wove its way through issues such as how many people were expected and numbers that the cathedral could hold. Paul insisted on screens throughout the nave and speakers outside in case the numbers swelled beyond capacity. Given that perhaps two thousand people might want to take communion, which could take up to half an hour, it was agreed that there would be helpers and volunteer ushers. The placement of television cameras and media was discussed, as well as flowers and Lifehouse donation envelopes.

We had already discussed eulogies and made our decisions. When planning the service, Dad had asked me if I would speak. Mum wondered whether she should also but he thought it would be too hard for her. In the days after he died Mum told me, 'I knew him better than anyone. I need to say something.' We had made plans for four others to speak at the cathedral: Dad's friend since childhood, Mark Malouf, would talk about schooldays and university life; Paul Cave would speak as his patient and Professor Michael Boyer as his colleague. Given the circumstances and their genuine friendship, it was appropriate for the prime minister to say something. Eventually a provisional order of service was agreed upon and, after two and a half hours, the group dispersed.

As Paul walked with us back to the car, he took a phone call on his mobile. 'We were just in there discussing it,' he said. He was raising his voice. 'We've just spent two and a half hours going through every single detail. If there was any possibility of an issue, then it should have been raised in the meeting.' Paul's voice was not calm and measured now. His face creased with frustration.

He pulled the phone away from his ear. 'Cardinal Pell has said that he won't permit six eulogies.'

'What?' Mum snapped. 'How many will he allow?'

'Only one.' We were shocked, not having contemplated the possibility that the head of the Catholic church in Australia would issue a command about something as personal as the eulogies for my father's funeral. 'Well, that's not going to happen,' Gail said. 'If that's the way it is, we'll take ourselves elsewhere.'

Paul seemed incensed. 'We were just in there. I asked if there were any concerns from the church's point of view and we were told no.'

'I'll go and see the cardinal,' Gail said.

The meeting was arranged in the offices of the Catholic Archdiocese of Sydney on the evening two days before the funeral. Gail was matter-of-fact about it, not inclined at this particular point in time to worry much about protocol or institutional demands.

The night before the meeting, Margaret Rose telephoned to offer her condolences. Margaret and her husband, Bob, an unpretentious property developer, had been generous benefactors of the Sydney Cancer Centre when Chris became director. They had insisted that our family spend a week at their palatial Palm Beach residence in January 2007, after Dad's first operation, moving themselves out so that we could stay there.

Gail told Margaret about the exhausting funeral arrangements and the issue with the eulogies. She said she was going to see the cardinal the next day.

'Darling, I think someone should go with you. I'll speak to Bob and see what he thinks.' She called back a short while later saying, 'Bob will go with you.'

It hadn't occurred to my mother that she should take someone more familiar with Catholic protocols than she was. As Bob and Gail made their way along the dark street towards Polding House the following evening, Gail felt a rush of gratitude that she was not doing this alone. Bob's fatherly manner, calm wisdom and experience in negotiations made her feel at ease. She was glad he was by her side.

They stepped into the large building and took the lift up several floors. They were greeted by Cardinal Pell's assistant and left to wait for a few minutes in large armchairs.

Cardinal Pell entered, his statuesque build filling the doorway. He was wearing a dark suit and clerical collar, and was warm but subdued as he greeted them. After several minutes, the conversation reached the real reason they were there. In her contained, composed manner and soft, delicate voice, Gail explained the problem of his edict to have only one eulogy at Chris's state funeral. Pell said that so many eulogies would interrupt the flow and reverence of the mass. Gail insisted that although six eulogists might seem excessive, we could not see how all the different facets of Dad's life could be celebrated appropriately otherwise. As the negotiations continued, Gail felt they had reached an impasse. But then Cardinal Pell volunteered a suggestion: he could potentially allow *three* eulogies. If the eulogists were paired up, a single eulogy might consist of two speakers, allowing all six to speak. These three joint eulogies should be spread out before and after the mass so that rather than interfering, the reflections would bookend the service. Gail was satisfied, although Pell gave no immediate assurance that he would permit this arrangement. But they had seemed to have reached an amicable resolution that everyone could live with.

'Eminence, Gail is a fairly feisty character,' Bob said in a light tone. 'Do you feel as though you've been hit by a bulldozer?'

'More like a truck,' Pell said drily, before inviting them to tour the new offices.

When Bob and Gail went to leave, Gail shook the cardinal's hand and thanked him. Bob stepped forward and asked whether he could kiss the cardinal's ring. Gail's mouth almost fell open as she was completely unfamiliar with this custom. Bob and Gail left the building, hugging each other. 'Don't worry,' said

Bob. 'It'll be okay.' Bob was right. Overnight the request was authorised by the Catholic Archdiocese of Sydney.

The opportunity to see Dad again came on the day before the funeral. His body was now at the funeral directors' premises in Newtown only a few hundred metres from the hospital room where he had died. It was disquieting to think of Dad's body being moved around. My mother's mind would drift to this thought. *Where is he now? Where is he lying? What are they doing to him?* This was the body she had lain next to for more than thirty years. The body that we had hugged and kissed. Somebody had him on level 10 of RPA or in the morgue, and someone else would have him the next day. Such thoughts indulge horror and are better not dwelt upon.

Mum drove Adam, James and me there and quietly manoeuvred the car into a nearby parking space on busy King Street. We were greeted by Patsy, the director of W.N. Bull who, along with her colleagues, could not have been more reassuring or empathetic. But nothing prepared us for what was to come. She showed us into the chapel, which was lit by a shaft of stark golden light from a small window. Even though there was an air of reverence, it felt eerie.

We had been told we could see Dad again, but he was not there. The face of the body we saw resembled that of our father but somehow it was different. The skin and eyes were sunken and the mouth was twisted into a grotesque smile. Stiff hands fell across his chest, with a red rose wedged between the fingers. Adam, James and Mum walked slowly down the aisle. Adam kissed the cold shiny forehead and Mum and James snipped off locks of hair.

'Come on, sweetie.' Mum held out her hand to me as I hovered between the pews. 'Come and say goodbye to Dad.'

'That's not Dad. That's not Dad,' I cried, and left the chapel to wait for them in the antechamber.

At home I secluded myself in my room. I just wanted darkness, stillness and quiet. But Mum pushed on. With nothing appropriate to wear for the funeral, her sister Adele and close friend Di took her to a shopping centre. She had remained so stoic over those previous few days, matter-of-factly organising the funeral, welcoming people into our home, meeting the cardinal, supporting us, her children. But seeing crowds of shoppers scavenging bargains at sales made her emotions overflow. *How could anyone care about towels?* she thought. On an escalator in the shopping centre, surrounded by the noise and energy of shoppers as they secured all kinds of allegedly desirable material goods, she broke down. Adele and Di took control, leading her to a change room and bringing her outfits one by one. Gail inspected the items through tears, eventually settling on a black Simona suit with a satin skirt and tailored jacket.

As quickly as she could she escaped the soulless centre, hurried home and climbed the stairs to her room. Her heart stabbed with pain. A real, physical pain that made her clutch her chest and gasp for breath. *Christie! Where are you, where are you, where are you?*

A State Funeral

When Sophia Loren's husband Carlo Ponti died about two years before Chris, pictures of the glamorous Loren appeared in the newspaper. The widow looked dour, wearing a long black coat and black scarf tight around her neck and her eyes were lowered to the ground. Gail thought Loren appeared diminished by her grief. She silently swore to herself then, that if the same day arrived for her, she would not appear like that.

On the day of the funeral, Pam arrived at the door at seven in the morning to blow-dry Gail's hair, just one example of a little physical attentiveness providing some help on this hard day. Gail went upstairs to her bathroom and began automatically selecting her make-up. She gazed hard at her reflection. 'I am *not* going to be a victim to this,' she said aloud. She dressed in the black suit and a beautiful, long, white coat lent to her for the day by Paul Cave's wife, Carol.

The black official state cars arrived at the house to collect us. They lined up like train carriages along our driveway. We stepped outside into the freezing Thursday morning under a brilliant blue sky. Our front gates had been laden with flowers by mourners who did not attach their names to them. The line of cars, accompanied by police officers on motorbikes, proceeded down Woolwich Road. Locals on their morning walks stopped and observed; a couple of old men removed their hats and held them to their chests.

We cruised along Victoria Road and turned onto the Anzac Bridge. There, we looked up at the Australian flags flying at half-mast at the bridge's peak. 'Oh, Dad,' Adam whispered. Uncle Phil later told Mum that all the flags at government schools were flying at half-mast also, and a friend sent us a photograph of the same on the Sydney Harbour Bridge.

We had always been proud of our father: when he spoke at my high-school graduation dinner and told us to avoid the cult of perfectionism, when he urged the boys at Parramatta Marist Brothers to understand that men of steel have compassion in their hearts, when he spoke to those at Riverview College of the importance of reading good literature to know more about other people's lives and experiences. We were as proud when he gave someone lip or made an irreverent remark as we were when he received his doctorate of medicine. But to see those flags flying at half-mast, showing that the nation mourned with us, that today we had all lost someone great, was a moment of overwhelming emotion. I thought of Phil's question again. *When did this happen?*

At the cathedral, we were shown into the chapter house. My mouth was dry and I felt exhausted. 'This is a nightmare,' I said, and started to weep.

'No it's not,' Mum said firmly. She bent down and took my hands. 'This is a wonderful day. We need to do this for Dad. All right? Do it for Dad.' I was momentarily taken aback by her strong voice and reaction. I nodded compliantly.

We had been given an order of arrangements with its minute-by-minute account of the dignitaries arriving:

> *9.40am Air Vice Marshal Mark Skidmore, representing the*
> *Chief of the Defence Force*
> *9.46am representatives of the diplomatic corps*
> *9.50am NSW Premier Nathan Rees*
> *9.52am Prime Minister Kevin Rudd*
> *9.54am Sir Nicholas Shehadie representing NSW Governor*
> *Marie Bashir*
> *9.56am Governor-General Quentin Bryce*

We entered the cathedral at 9.58am. Patsy and Father Paul, the dean of St Mary's, greeted us at the cathedral entrance. As we walked down the long aisle that stretched out before us, I saw Mum's steady gaze. She looked down the long nave to the altar where Dad's coffin lay draped with the Australian flag and his favourite flowers, irises and white oriental lilies. The fragrance of the lilies reached us as we approached. Keith Cox hugged each of us and showed us to our seats. He moved back up to the altar, seeming to float as his white acolyte robes hid his feet.

Behind us, the pews were full and many people were standing. They were people from all over Sydney and even the world: Dad's former trainees and fellows, past patients, colleagues, friends and people who had not known him personally but who had come to pay their respects.

The introductory hymn rang out. 'Praise my soul the king of heaven', boys from Parramatta Marist Brothers and St Ignatius' College, Riverview sang. Their resonant voices boomed through the nave as more than a dozen priests and Cardinal Pell made their way down the aisle. I caught Father Kev's eye and he gave me a wink before they all moved around the altar. Cardinal Pell presided over the service.

The national anthem followed the hymn. Father Kev welcomed everyone, his words echoing through the great space that felt warm from all the bodies. He moved around the casket, blessed it and sprinkled it with holy water. Keith Cox floated in front of us to collect the first eulogists.

Cardinal Pell had requested seeing the text of all the eulogies before the day. 'As far as the cardinal is concerned, my talk won't be ready until the day of the service,' Kevin Rudd had responded. But Mark Malouf had obliged and was subsequently asked to shorten his speech. Professor Michael Boyer spoke, describing Chris as a 'surgeon's surgeon'. Paul Cave shed tears as he said that he would have gone in Chris's stead, had he been given the choice.

The mass began. My father's aunt Alison Healey stepped out of her seat and approached the altar for the first reading, from the Book of Proverbs. She had suggested this reading, which I'd not thought much about until this moment. She read purposefully and deliberately, pausing at words and phrases, allowing them to hang in the air.

> *A perfect wife is far beyond the price of pearls;*
> *her husband's heart trusts in her;*
> *from her he will derive no little profit;*
> *advantage, not hurt, she brings him*
> *all the days of her life.*
> *She works with her hands in delight;*
> *she gives food to her household;*
> *she puts her back into her work;*
> *and shows how strong her arms can be;*
> *she finds her labour well worthwhile;*
> *her lamp does not go out at night.*

I looked at my mother. Her face was almost serene, her lips turned up at the corners in the most pleasant neutral expression anyone could have. She sat with her feet square on the floor and hands folded in her lap. No pretences. No acting. She just sat and listened.

The second reading was given by the governor-general, Quentin Bryce, and Her Excellency made her way up to the lectern, looking strikingly elegant as always. She read from the First Letter of Paul to the Corinthians. Though her voice was not strong, her slow and deliberate reading commanded the cathedral.

Though I command languages both human and angelic — if I speak without love, I am no more than a gong booming or a cymbal clashing. And though I have the power of prophecy, to penetrate all mysteries and knowledge, and though I have all the faith necessary to move mountains — if I am without love, I am nothing.

The voices of the combined choirs boomed through the cathedral. *Alleluia, Alleluia.* Aunt Alison stood, the centre of expanding concentric circles as everyone around her copied each other. Father James Collins read the Gospel and Father Kev gave a personal and emotional homily, having walked closely with us on this path. Young women and men whom my father loved — my cousins and dear family friends — offered gifts as Mozart's 'Ave Verum' filled our ears and hearts.

Father Kev caught my eye again. He upturned his hands and pushed upward like a shelf. *Stand.* I stood. He said the Eucharistic Prayer. The organ shattered the air. I looked intently at Father Kev as he pushed his hands down. I bent towards the pew. Later he would tell me that from the altar it looked like a wave moving through the sea as row after row of people joined those in front.

Finally it was time for communion, with a precious moment to sit quietly while the choirs sang. Out of the many faces emerged individual friends who collected by the altar and dispersed to the corners of the cathedral to act as eucharistic ministers. It was beautiful to see friends from our dear parish helping us in that gentle way, a hint of the support and organisation that had gone on behind the scenes, a lot of it without our knowledge. Not many people took communion after it was announced that non-Catholics should approach with their arms folded to indicate that they be blessed instead. Most people seemed content to watch the flat screens that had come alive with images of Dad's life. People chuckled at old pictures of furry moustaches and orange tans.

As I returned from taking communion and knelt onto the soft knee rest at our pew, I wanted to let the music carry me away. Villa Maria musicians, Harrison Collins and Lee Liao, sang Andrew Lloyd Webber's 'Pie Jesu — Requiem'. Then Harrison picked up his violin and, accompanied by Lee, Rolf Lovland, Brendan Graham, Thomas De Angelis and Bernadette Galea, sang Dad's favourite hymn, 'You raise me up'. Sublime and laden with symbolism, the 'you' in this song is supposed to be God. But for Adam, James and me, the figure who raised us up was our father. For Mum, it was her husband. And for others in that cathedral, it was their brother, nephew, son-in-law, mentor and friend. Chris, Christie, Dad, had always raised us up. He had worked so hard in his life. In death, he would keep raising us up.

The prayer after communion concluded the mass, and Keith moved down the steps to collect the last eulogists, my mother and me. It was my turn to speak first, and I felt too numb to be nervous. The night before the service I had read out what I had written to my boyfriend, Gareth. 'It's a really good start,' he had said with gentle encouragement. At 11pm and having considered it finished, it was not what I had wanted to hear. But Gareth had helped me to keep writing, and by the next day, the words seemed to lift off the page on their own.

'My dad was wise, but youthful. He was respectful but irreverent. He had incredible willpower, but an insuperable sweet tooth. He was a leader. He was an equal. He maintained that we are all the same, just at different stages of our lives and careers. He demanded excellence of himself, but only wanted us kids to do our best. If our best produced excellence, all the better. He was our father and our friend. He was my best friend.'

When Mum stepped forward, she was completely composed. 'My name is Gail O'Brien,' she began. As she spoke, her voice did not break once. She seemed stronger than ever, as though being supported by an unseen force. 'It actually took great stamina, patience and a certain cunning to be married to Chris,' she said to muffled chuckles. 'But the last two and a half years brought us even closer together than either of us could ever have imagined.' She described those last days and thanked those people who had been so important. 'For all of us, may our tears of grief be replaced by tears of joy at having known such a man. He raises us all up to higher standards of selflessness and goodness towards our fellow man.

'Christie, I know that you are revered in heaven even more than you were revered on earth. Until we meet again, the children and I will walk in your footprints and continue to be inspired by you, my honeybun, my Dr Gorgeous.'

It was over. The pallbearers took their places around the coffin that we had chosen. It was a modest casket as befitted a man from humble beginnings, of light-coloured wood and with wooden handles, not too much shiny brass. Patsy had been concerned about the pallbearers carrying it all the way down the cathedral aisle. 'It's a long walk,' she had said, but Gail had insisted, 'I want Chris to be carried.' Patsy lined up eight men who were so dear in Dad's life, keeping the shorter and taller together, and supervised as they heaved the casket onto their shoulders.

'Right foot first,' she said in a low, firm voice. And they led us out into the bleached daylight. Old friends from Marist Brothers led a cheer and the crowd clapped as the hearse rolled away. It was a glorious end to an extraordinary life.

Everybody went to Guillaume's restaurant at the Sydney Opera House for the wake. 'Now, *this* is a party!' Mum yelled to us over her shoulder with a grin as we entered. She led the way through a mass of moving shoulders and faces, hands holding champagne glasses and extending for hors d'oeuvres. People wearing suits and dresses in black, navy and grey wedged themselves onto the balcony and the top floor, and cascaded down the stairs into the main body of the restaurant. The room roared with noise as guests shouted, laughed and cried, draping their arms around one another, clinking glasses and wiping away tears. Decades of friends and acquaintances brought with them Chris's entire life.

We family members were the last to arrive, having come from Macquarie Park crematorium. A few hundred of us had proceeded to the more intimate chapel setting, where Carmel and Dad's brother, Mike, had given eulogies. Carmel and Phil's son Matthew had played 'Fields of gold' on guitar. Col Joye sang and played 'Just a closer walk with Thee' while Father Kev improvised jazz piano riffs to accompany him. They finished with 'Somewhere over the rainbow' — encouraging the chapel to join in. The chapel service beautifully complemented the reverential authority of St Mary's Cathedral.

Now we were at the wake in the midst of a wild, roaring bash, generously hosted by Guillaume. The microphone was passed around freely, and stories about Chris were met with a combination of raucous laughter and tears. When Michael Besser began to speak, his solemn tones hushed the crowd. He read 'Invictus' by William Ernest Henley.

Out of the night that covers me,
Black as the pit from pole to pole,
I thank whatever gods may be
For my unconquerable soul.
In the fell clutch of circumstance
I have not winced nor cried aloud.
Under the bludgeonings of chance
My head is bloody, but unbowed.
Beyond this place of wrath and tears
Looms but the Horror of the shade,
And yet the menace of the years
Finds, and shall find, me unafraid.
It matters not how strait the gate,
How charged with punishments the scroll,
I am the master of my fate,
I am the captain of my soul.

Gail sat on a dark cushioned seat that curved along the wall next to the speakers. Chris was all around her. She heard a rowdy group on the balcony above — Chris's friends from medical school and Royal Prince Alfred Hospital. 'He would have loved to be here,' one of them said. But she felt that he was.

Kevin Rudd went and sat beside her. 'I want to ask your permission for something, Gail. Lifehouse should be named after Chris. Will you give your permission for it to be the Chris O'Brien Cancer Centre?' Gail had not been surprised to hear

Chris discussed on breakfast television on the morning after his death. Nor was the offer of a state funeral unexpected. Once again she was unsurprised. She and Chris had briefly talked about this possibility. 'I just don't want my name on a lemon,' he had told her. A vestige of these words lay in her memory.

'Yes, of course,' she told the prime minister instantly, thrilled at the thought of Chris's name living on in bricks and mortar, a glorious testament to what he had lived for. Kevin Rudd put his arm around her. When the speaker finished, Mr Rudd stood up and reached for the microphone. 'I've just been chatting here with Gail. She has agreed to have Lifehouse named after Chris. From now on, it will be known as the Chris O'Brien Cancer Centre at RPA.' Cheers erupted as the crowd agreed it was right.

Though Gail could not have known it at the time, her consent had shifted the tectonic plates under her life. By agreeing to this honour — and how could she not agree? — Gail had unknowingly burdened herself with an onerous responsibility. The task of honouring Chris's name, guarding his vision, making sure that his name didn't end up on 'a lemon' would be immense. It would be all-consuming. The decision had been easy. Its consequences would prove extreme.

Where is My Husband?

We arrived home at the end of that day entirely depleted. With the funeral over and our lives without Dad yawning before us, we yearned for the burden of caring again. It was a period of acute grief, which felt much like an illness itself. At times the mental anguish made Mum think she was going mad. One day as she was coming down the stairs to the front foyer she distinctly heard Chris's voice say, 'Pinkie.' She looked around for him as naturally as if he were standing right there behind her. It wouldn't have surprised her if he had been, his voice was that clear and strong.

The impetus to continue living life through these months displaying some guise of normalcy is strong but misguided. Gail continued *doing*. In hindsight, we should just have focused on *being*.

Gail had tickets to see the guitarist Tommy Emmanuel at the Angel Place recital hall. Chris had loved Tommy Emmanuel and they'd bought the tickets months beforehand. Now, ten days after his funeral, Gail gave Chris's ticket to her friend Di. Gail wanted to listen to the music Chris had loved, but now it seemed pointless, like everything else. She was just going through the motions; trying to be part of a life to which she felt no connection.

At the end of June she had an appointment with a dermatologist. At a regular skin check a few months before, the dermatologist pointed out that she had broken capillaries on her cheeks. She couldn't have cared less at the time, but made an appointment to have the capillaries lasered. Now that day had come around, and she went. When she returned home, Adam, James and I were horrified to see how badly bruised her cheeks were. They became a deep purple colour and she was putting ice on her face for days. Having her capillaries lasered was a strange thing to do at such a time — we recognise this now. We have since speculated that it was almost a form of self-harm, a way to externalise pain that had built up inside.

Everybody was kind and tried to pretend, or assumed, that Gail's life was returning to normal. Friends suggested she go on a holiday, as if to say, 'It's over now so you can take a break.' Many asked her for coffee. Within weeks of Chris's death, a friend who was not particularly close invited her to an art class. Gail obliged and they agreed to have dinner afterwards. Even in those first raw weeks, she felt pressure to get back into life and do something to extend herself. The art studio was a ten-minute drive from her friend's house and Gail offered to drive them both there. The still-life sketching and painting lessons were pleasant enough, but not the chatter of the students, who were oblivious to Gail's inner torment. As the night went on Gail felt worse and worse. She knew she had made a mistake in agreeing to this; all she wanted was to be in the nurturing environment of our home. After class she endured a meal at a noisy Thai restaurant and drove home via her friend's house, but the woman continued to sit in the car chatting. Gail felt like screaming, 'Get out of the car!' but didn't want to offend this lady, whose intentions had, after all, been good. Gail finally escaped and fled home, exhausted, and went to her room and wept, overwhelmed with grief, pain, heartache and hopelessness.

All we could do as a family was to stay close to home and be together. Home was a sanctuary; we all depended on each other to get ourselves through. Carmel and Phil stayed with us for a few more weeks. They cooked dinner and made us laugh. It was a wrench when they had to go back to their own place on the south coast, but they drove up to see us regularly. At the end of July they came up for Mum's birthday, helping me to celebrate by giving her cups of tea and presents in bed in the morning. Adam would come over later in the day, and I preferred to let James sleep longer that morning. At night, we went for dinner at a local Chinese restaurant. When the fortune cookies arrived, we all took one and read out the fortunes. Mum's was, 'You are going to have a very long life.' The entire table groaned: loudest of all, wearing a sardonic smile, was Mum. A long life? Right now that was the last thing she wanted.

About a month after the state funeral our parish held a more intimate mass for Dad. Gail spoke again at this service but this time she was less composed. 'The day following Chris's death,' she said, 'a learned friend drew our attention to theology, in an attempt to answer that unfathomable question.' She looked at me and began to cry at the pulpit. 'Where is my husband now?'

The 'learned friend' was Kevin Rudd, who had telephoned to ask how we all were. The boys were stoic and I was not, so he asked to speak with me. I nervously took the phone, feeling anxious about speaking with the prime minister. But the twenty-minute conversation was warm and flowing. He told me how painful it had been when he lost his own mother, and how much solace he had drawn from the exercise of seeking out a beautiful cupboard and placing her most precious keepsakes in it.

'You're probably asking yourself, "Where is my father now?"' he said.

'Yes,' I whispered.

'There is a passage in the Gospel, the book of John, that addresses this question. It says, "In my Father's house are many rooms: if it were not so, I would have told you. I go to prepare a place for you." We cannot understand or even fathom this concept, of many rooms. Whether you believe in God or not, what is certain is that something happened in Jerusalem a little more than 2000 years ago, which caused ripples across the world.'

As Mr Rudd spoke about these practical and spiritual questions of death, clearing his throat intermittently as he talked, I felt a little buoyed by the prospect of a clear and tangible task in finding a precious cupboard. And I deeply appreciated his scholarly contribution to the questions with which I was indeed grappling — where had my father and his love gone?

One cold night I lay by the fire, listening to the recording of the radio interview Dad had done just before his last operation. Adam came and sat beside me, rubbing his knuckles as he had done since he was a boy. James joined us. Mum came in to find us together, flat and wallowing in the chasm. She lit a beautiful, thick, white candle her sister-in-law Lyndall had given to us. It was a memorial candle with an image of Dad printed onto it, and it burned slowly and assuredly, as if it would never reach the bottom.

'Look at that flame,' Mum said, as she placed the candle on the coffee table between us. 'It's there but at the same time it's not there. I can see it, yet run my finger through it. What is to say that Dad isn't like that flame?' The three of us stayed silent. 'Dad would not have left us,' Mum said, defiant, willing us to know what she felt was the truth. 'He loved us too much to leave us. And I'm going to find him.'

* * *

Family lore has it that Gail's grandmother Franny Bamford once had a premonition. Her cousin Hal had emigrated from Ireland to Canada, but he and Franny remained close, keeping in contact by letter. At the outbreak of World War I, Hal enlisted in the Canadian armed forces and was sent to France. Weeks later he appeared to Franny in a dream, standing by her bed then reaching out and touching her arm.

'Hal's dead,' Franny said to her husband when she woke up. 'He came to me in my sleep.' She pulled her arm out from under the covers and showed the place where Hal had touched her. The skin was burning red hot.

'Don't tell anyone,' Franny's husband said. 'Everyone will think you're mad.'

But in a matter of days the news indeed arrived that Hal had been killed. Call it intuition, Irish superstition, a family fable embellished through the generations. When told by my mother or grandfather the story is usually followed by a thin smile and unblinking eyes, as if to say, 'It could be true. Who are you to say otherwise?'

Following the service at Villa Maria, Gail was talking to a group of people just outside the door of the chapter hall when a kind-faced Indian woman with wild black hair took her hand and introduced herself. Her name was Veronica. She pressed her phone number into Gail's hand and asked her to call. Gail couldn't wait to ring. She was at the beginning of a journey in which any lead had to be followed. That evening, she closed the study door and dialled the number. 'Today you asked, where is your husband. I felt that I had to respond,' said Veronica. She explained that she had worked at Prince Alfred in the laboratory and had known Chris. She had great faith in God. She described peculiar experiences following the death of a close family member — explicit dreams and signs that she said were more than coincidence.

A few days later, Gail went to Veronica's home, where the woman served tea and shared her spiritual beliefs. 'Chris is in a place where there is no more pain and no more tears,' she said. She suggested that they recite the Lord's Prayer together.

Gail appreciated the gesture and kindness, but she needed so much more. And she didn't know exactly where to turn.

Soon after Adam had started attending St Ignatius' College, Riverview, a large Jesuit college for boys, a fellow mother told Gail that she attended mass every day. 'If I don't go, I just don't feel right,' the woman said. Gail was impressed by her devotion, but she didn't fully understand it.

Raised Presbyterian, Gail occasionally felt something of an outsider at St Ignatius'.

Adam, James and I had all been baptised Catholic and gone through the sacraments of reconciliation, communion and confirmation. It felt a natural choice for Chris and Gail to raise their children this way, with Chris having had a strongly Catholic upbringing. Our chosen confirmation names were illustrative of our young outlooks. So enamoured was he with the name Christopher, Adam chose that, even though it was already his Christian name. I happily took my grandmother's advice of adopting the name Cecilia, the patron saint of music. James chose Saint Bartholomew for no other reason than being inspired by *The Simpsons* cartoon character Bart.

Until I was about ten years old, Dad would take Adam and me to mass on Sundays, which we welcomed as it was usually followed by a treat of *pain au chocolat*. But as we children grew older and life got busier, the family attended mass less frequently.

When I was about thirteen years old, Mum announced that she was converting to Catholicism. When Gail told her mother about her plans, Grace said, 'I don't know why you would bother. It's all incense, bells and fuss.' At the time, I did not understand my mother's reasons. But I see now that, while there had been no need for Gail to convert before marrying Chris (as both of them considered this anachronistic), my mother appreciated the traditions, sense of celebration and community offered by the Catholic church — and our local parish in particular. She wanted the family to enjoy these together.

Mum's desire for the family to celebrate together was never fully realised. In his teenage years, James told us that he did not believe in God. I think Adam's faith and connection to his Catholic upbringing were strong, but his shift work meant mass attendance was a rare occurrence. As I matured, I found that my own attitude to mass was similar to Dad's: it was an opportunity to spend one hour connected to some kind of spirituality, meditating on something greater than one's self. Now, my (irregular) attendance is driven by an agnostic openness and desire to support and be connected with the parish community, rather than any deeply held faith.

Going to mass had answered a longing in Gail that she could not quite articulate. Perhaps her decision to convert is best summed up by the Christian philosopher and mathematician Blaise Pascal: 'The heart has its reasons of which reason knows nothing.'

But as important as mass was to her, at this point in her life she desperately needed more. Eventually she would find nourishment both within and outside of the conventions of the church.

Like her grandmother, Gail seemed to find something more during sleep. Facing bed alone she was prompted to rummage through the meditation CDs sitting by the stereo. She found one called 'Mental Resilience: A guided relaxation'. The disc is an accompaniment to the book by Kamal Sarma, an international management consultant and fund manager who writes that he resorted to the lessons he learned in an Indian ashram following the death of his baby daughter. Gail climbed back into bed as the CD began to spin. This time she lay on Chris's side of the bed. They had slept in the same formation for close to thirty years — his right shoulder touching her left. In order to feel closer to him, she simply lay in his place.

The CD did its job. Gail listened, stilled her mind without too much trouble and drifted into sleep. Listening to the CD became a daily habit. As the weeks after Chris's death became months, she did this unfailingly every night. And as is common with habits, the more she practised, the better she became.

One night, Gail lay there not quite asleep but not fully awake when there was a sudden shift in her senses. She felt as if her body was moving forward, as though she was in an accelerating car. The two-dimensional blackness behind her closed eyelids turned into three-dimensional darkness, like a black void. It became dotted with stars. Brighter and brighter they shone. She was in the night sky. It happened the next night too, and again soon after that, until night after night she would enter this space. It became so reliable that it would be as if it arrived to collect her. Expecting it, she would lie in bed and wait. And then she would stay in the sky until she drifted into sleep.

As this ritual continued, she began to see more than stars. There were faces in that void, milky faces that looked like holograms or x-rays. She didn't recognise them and some were frightening. But one night she saw Chris's face — blurred and undefined; present but distant. 'Christie,' she said. He didn't reply and drew away into the dark void again.

Gail knew she couldn't tell many people about these metaphysical travels each night. She confided in Dominique, a trusted friend who is also a spiritual director. Gail had known Dominique as a devout member of the parish, but through many conversations had learned that her friend's spiritual life transcended the concept of 'a judgmental grandfather in the sky'. Gail described the faces. Dominique smiled. 'Like looking through a glass darkly,' she said, referring to a phrase from Paul's famous letter to the Corinthians.

One night, after her flights, Gail dreamed about a diamond ring Chris had bought for her. She had misplaced it and had been looking everywhere for it, simultaneously scrambling for those tangible memories she could hold on to yet reminding herself of the insignificance of material possessions. As she prepared for bed that night, she asked Chris to help her find it. Then, in her dream, she saw the ring. It was standing upright and shining in a rose-coloured light. The next day while getting dressed, she looked at her pink dressing gown hanging on the back of the door and peered into its slim pocket. There was the ring, resting in an upright position, glowing in the pink fabric. She clutched it in her hand and pressed it against her heart. 'Thank you, thank you, thank you,' she whispered.

Gail was well on her way on a spiritual journey that took her outside of the walls of a church. Affirmations that perhaps Chris was not so remote were finding their way to her. After making a speech at a retirement village in the northern suburbs about her and Chris's experiences, a woman approached her with tears in her eyes. 'On the way here, I heard Chris,' the stranger said. 'He said, "I'm always with my wife."' At a dinner with Chris's past colleagues, a New Zealand woman whispered, 'Chris is here,' waving her fingers over Gail's head and shoulders. 'I can feel him.'

Gail took her father to South Cronulla beach and he sat on a bench while she walked over the rocks. She was feeling fragile and her eyes welled with tears in the fresh sea air. *Christie, please send me a sign, send me a sign*, she thought. She considered a story she had read in which the writer had drawn meaning from a feather found on a beach. She looked around. *Don't bother about feathers, they don't mean anything to me*, she thought. The next day was a scorcher and the stifling air was still. Gail called out to Adam as she walked through the dining room and felt something underfoot. She stopped and looked down. It was a long, perfect feather, yellow and white in colour. 'What's the matter? What's wrong?' Adam came in after hearing his mother gasp. Gail had the feather in her hands. 'That's from a cockatoo,' he said. 'How'd that get in here?'

Gail was sceptical of signs, but what was she to make of these people and events? The rational mind could easily dismiss them as coincidences and some weirdos. If these were signs, then of what? 'That's what spiritual direction is,' Dominique told her. 'It's noticing. Noticing the Spirit communicating with you.'

Years earlier, shortly after Gail had converted to Catholicism and was regularly attending mass at Villa Maria, a young, dynamic priest visited from the USA. He spoke to the parish and said, 'There are no coincidences, they're all Godincidences.' That had stuck in Gail's mind. Through her relationship with Dominique she was returning to this idea. They discussed coincidences, awareness and noticing, Jungian synchronicities and the opportunities at connectivity, that these are moments that are ever-present, if one is open to them. There is a choice to brush them off as chance or probability, or to notice them and tacitly accept them as a part of a current running underneath the water's surface.

Dominique suggested that Gail speak to someone about her noticings, someone who could offer pastoral support as well as guidance. She recommended Sister Pauline, a spiritual director at Mary MacKillop Place in North Sydney. Sister Pauline had trained Dominique, who had great respect for and trust in her. Gail made the appointment and found the little elderly nun sitting in a pew at the back of the church. She followed the woman out of the church and through a maze of corridors in the residential area. They entered a small, stark room, with a high window that revealed the sky.

It was the first of monthly sessions over the next year, in which Sister Pauline's gentle questioning led to emotional outpourings of grief. A box of tissues nearby identified that this was common.

At the end of one session, Sister Pauline asked, 'So what is it that you want, Gail?'

Gail looked out the window thoughtfully. 'I want to be struck dumb with the awe of it.'

Sister Pauline smiled. 'No one's ever said that to me before.'

My dear Mum,

I struggle to 'notice' things like you do, or appreciate small details of life as signs of some greater force. I do not deter you from your journey, but I do not accompany you either.

As we share your story with anyone who will listen, is there anything that you'd like to say to them — and to me?

All my love, Juliette

* * *

My darling,

I have been reluctant to tell people about my experiences, fearing how I would be judged. Would I be humiliated? Would people not take me seriously?

I would be a deserter if I didn't tell it the way it is. A deserter of the many people who have similar experiences, and a deserter of the truth.

'Just tell the truth', is what Thomas Merton said, and I know what the truth is.

From Richard Rohr: 'Be prepared to be humiliated at least once every day.' And I am!

My darling, all that I can do is invite you to suspend judgment. Suspend judgment, Juliette. That is all you need to do.

Love, Mum

Asking the Questions

When Patsy brought us Dad's ashes a few days after he was cremated, she held the cedar box with reverence. 'He had heavy bones,' she said to Gail. We placed the box in the living room and made plans to place the ashes in the garden.

A few months later, on Father's Day 2009, the extended family gathered with us to do this. At the far end of the lawn, sandstone steps led down to a private little area with a curved seat, azaleas, agapanthus and a statue of a small boy gazing down. We would place Dad's ashes there, but only for the time being; if we ever moved house we would have to take them with us.

'You're going to have to put them in something watertight then,' Gail's mother told her. So Gail went to Bunnings in search of an appropriate vessel.

'You're after an Esky?' a smiling young man asked, as she studied the range.

'Um, yes,' said Gail. *Please don't ask what it's for.*

Phil, Mike and Gail's brother Murray worked together as the heavy, bony ashes were removed from the cedar box and, still within their plastic casing, placed in the Esky. They sealed the edges and dug a good-sized hole among the agapanthus. Aunt Alison read a poem and guided us in a small ceremony. We laid Dad's ashes down and covered them over with earth, placing small ornaments beside them. The statue of the boy gazed over them and later a rose bush was planted over the spot where they lay. It soon produced tiny delicate yellow roses. It was a small, peaceful, sacred corner of the world.

We found ourselves clinging to Dad's possessions. His work shirts. His jackets and shoes. Even his Blackberry mobile phone took on a precious quality. Just nineteen years old, James had not cried freely until a simple but tangible loss brought him undone. The hospital band he had taken from around Chris's wrist had disappeared, possibly thrown out by a cleaner who swept through his room. James was distraught at the loss of this simple object; the real loss of his dad surely lay behind his tears.

Gail put Chris's aftershave in its elegant bottle beside her bed. She would breathe in the familiar fragrance to make him feel close. Scraps of paper with his handwriting couldn't be thrown out. I have one today in which Dad's pen has written 'Births and Deaths' across the top. 'George Washington 1732 — 1799, Mark Twain 1835 — 1910', the list goes on. Was it a mental exercise, I wonder. But beside each date is a number: 67,

75; how many years they lived. Nearing the end of his own life, was he reflecting on the longevity of others? These are the kinds of meditations that such physical objects provoke. It's as if your loved one has become a historical figure and you're searching for clues to their existence.

People would ask Gail to go for walks but she chose to walk alone. She took long treks with Mr Menzies through Kelly's Bush — a patch of bushland on the Hunters Hill peninsula that had been saved from development in Sydney's first green ban. The bush was healing for her and she was very thankful to the women and men who had ensured that it remained. The smell of trees, moist grass, wattle, gum leaves and eucalypts, the sounds of the birds, the aloneness, the quiet. She never wanted to run into someone she knew and would venture off the beaten track to avoid it. She would sit on a log on the ground and let the bush speak to her.

On one of these walks, along a tiny track she had walked several times, she came across a unique and magical-looking tree. It rose up magnificently in the middle of the bush and was completely covered in fungus. Toadstools sprouted and shone from every inch of the giant. Then Gail saw it was not one tree, but two. One large bole was anchored into the earth and two distinct trunks grew out of it, leaning on each other as they stretched up to the sky. Always on the lookout for messages, Gail found one here. The tree spoke to her: *We are still two, together as one.*

That day as she picked up the pace to get home she rolled her ankle, the same one she had injured tumbling down the stairs in the QVB. She hobbled home, which exacerbated the injury, and by the time I arrived hours later she couldn't put her foot anywhere near the floor without pulsating pain. I found her in bed with her foot propped on several cushions. She tried to move and, nimble as ever, slid off the bed, flipped onto one knee and then back onto her elbows, all while holding her sore foot high in the air. She wasn't amused when I joked that she looked as if she was doing some weird contemporary dance routine. A week later she limped into a kitchen store in search of a new dishwasher. The store owner, an elegant Frenchwoman, asked what was wrong. When Gail explained that she had sprained her ankle, the woman said, 'Come, sit and put it up. I can help you.'

Gail sat and felt awkward in this peculiar situation — surrounded by display kitchens with a stranger massaging her foot. She confided, 'My husband died recently, so everything seems harder than usual.'

'But he is still here,' said the woman. 'They're only on the other side of the curtain.'

The woman's husband appeared through a doorway and asked what she was doing. *'Mal au pied!'* she snapped. He shrugged his shoulders and left, as though he had walked out of the back office many times to find his wife whispering intensely to a stranger while giving a foot massage.

'I have a healing class that I go to,' the Frenchwoman said. 'You should come. There are very special people who come to this.' Gail went to the healing class in a small apartment in Willoughby. She was told that it was energetic healing, a therapy that claims to use the body's energy circuits to facilitate natural healing mechanisms. About ten people were there. They all seemed genial enough, and although Gail found the therapy that involved tapping on her acupressure points relaxing, she didn't go back.

My mother's inability to believe that her husband's love could simply evaporate had set her on a course in which she couldn't shun opportunities for unorthodox methods of healing, which seemed to find her regularly. Determined to be open-minded, she would say yes to many different things and occasionally ended up in some strange situations. One invitation presented itself via an unlikely avenue: Lyndall, Gail's sister-in-law and a self-described atheist who is equally intolerant of traditional religion and new-age spirituality. Lyndall told Gail that she'd heard about a Maori woman on the Central Coast who was said to be a spiritualist with incredible clairvoyant abilities.

When Lyndall asked whether Gail would like to see this woman, Gail didn't hesitate. The two of them drove to a sleepy beachside suburb north of Sydney. The house was a modest weatherboard cottage on the corner of the main road. Lyndall knocked on the front door, which was answered by a petite grandmotherly woman with short white hair. She looked directly at Gail.

'Someone's died! Your father!' she exclaimed.

'No, no,' Gail stumbled and started to back away. She was reluctant to go inside and looked at Lyndall, who said, 'I'll do my session first.'

'Could you please tell me if there's a coffee shop nearby where I can wait?' Gail asked, but the woman standing in the doorway appeared confused and distracted. Her response was incoherent and she flicked her hand vaguely. The door closed and Gail turned around, wondering what she had got herself into. She wandered around for an hour, passing small, identical houses and old, battered shops. She returned to the cottage, sat on its wooden verandah and felt in her pocket for Chris's rosary beads. *Please come to me, Christie*, she whispered, cupping the beads in her hands.

Lyndall appeared. 'It's your turn.'

'Hello dear, I'm Suzy,' said the woman as Gail stepped into the house. Suzy had a New Zealand accent and her manner had completely changed. 'I'm sorry about before. There was so much noise in my ear! Someone was trying to get my attention. Kept on and on at me.'

Gail had heard nothing and didn't understand what Suzy was talking about. They entered a small hallway and turned into a dimly lit room on the right. There was a small square table in the centre with two chairs facing each other and a sofa to the side. A tape recorder sat on the table. Suzy showed Gail to one of the chairs. Gail looked over her left shoulder and saw a mirror hanging on the wall.

Suzy sat down and began to pray in Maori. She then looked over Gail's shoulder into the mirror and appeared to start having a conversation. She was calling someone Florence and explained to Gail that this was Suzy's grandmother. The conversation continued, and then Suzy said, 'Okay, so Chris is in the hallway now.'

Gail's heart began to race. Sure, she had been speaking to Chris and even praying to him just moments before. But she didn't actually believe that he was there.

'Be careful, Chris,' Suzy said. Gail turned her head over her shoulder and looked towards the mirror. She saw nothing.

'How did you find me, love?' Suzy asked. Gail opened her mouth to answer, but Suzy put her hand up and looked into the mirror.

'Yes, I can hear you, Chris.' She started repeating what Chris was saying, but it was a string of non sequiturs that moved between first person and third.

'Oh, you've moved to Chris's side of the bed.'

Gail froze. 'Yes, I have.'

'Chris says that's good. He can reach you more easily there. I see a fountain in a garden. There's a stone, curved seat. That's where his ashes are. Chris says he's going to change the colour of the roses. Don't do anything, he will change the colour.'

Gail began to laugh and cry at once. Suzy continued, '2010 will be punctuated by Gail. You will make an impact. I'm right by her side. I have him in spirit. Life is an adventure. This is for

Gail. This is for Gail to find out what her vocation in life should be. Chris was on a mission in life, almost running; you will make a quiet impact. Not done by yelling and screaming.'

And then the session was over. It felt as if it had lasted just a few minutes but Gail looked at her watch and saw that two hours had passed. Suzy was sweating profusely. They walked out to the verandah where Lyndall was waiting.

As they drove home, they shared with each other what had happened in that room. Gail asked Lyndall, 'Did you give Suzy any information about me?'

'I didn't even tell her your name. I used my first name to make the booking.'

During the following months, Gail spoke to Suzy regularly. She told Suzy that she felt better for having done so, and Suzy assured her that she felt the same way about Gail. Suzy refused payment so often that it felt as if she and Gail were friends more than anything else.

After that first meeting with Suzy, Gail's enquiry into faith, spirituality and consciousness became all-consuming. Her search for meaning became vast, meandering and at times frenetic, and it took her to many places. She learned about the international Jain communities practising the reformation of Brahmanic Hindu tradition, was immersed in the Buddhism of Bhutan and discovered Santa Fe in New Mexico — the city of St Francis of Assisi — where leaders in Judaism, Buddhism and Christianity came together for a meeting of minds on paths to spiritualism.

She learned about central Australia and New Zealand, exploring respective Indigenous spiritualities and investigated the spiritual teachings of the Essenes, the knowledge of the kabbalah and the collective unconscious.

But perhaps the greatest application of everything she learned was at mass, where she came to understand the rituals in the context of ancient traditions. More than 'incense, bells and fuss', she saw the sweet-smelling smoke emanating from the swinging thurible as not unlike the smoking ceremonies of Australia's Aboriginal peoples or Native American Indians. The priest's laying on of hands to call down the Holy Spirit, the pervasive concept of light, the use of holy oils — it is all interconnected with the ideas of consciousness and spirit that she had explored and experienced.

As time passed she knew she was getting stronger. She didn't have to cling any more.

When the first anniversary of Chris's death arrived, we marked it with loving family and friends, laughing and sharing memories, while making new ones in each other's company. The same little rose bush over Dad's ashes now had roses in bloom that were a pinkish colour, not yellow. They had indeed changed. We were buoyed. We had survived.

But the universe was not done with us yet.

Christopher Adam

Adam, my elder brother and Gail's first-born child, was a strapping, affable young man. As a child he had angelic features of blond hair and blue eyes, and in his twenties he was good-looking in a rugged style. He usually had a few days of rough stubble on his chin and one front tooth was slightly darker than the other, having had it capped after he broke it falling off his skateboard as a child. While James and I inherited our father's dark colouring, blond hair covered Adam's arms, chest and back. He spoke with a broad Australian accent.

Adam cultivated his brawny physique by means of weights and resistance training. He lifted 160 kilograms on his bench press and worked his 'door gym' until it squeaked. The sound of metal clinking against metal and the occasional crash as weights fell to the floor meant Adam was home. His powerful build made his presence in a room known, even though he was of average height. As a teenager sitting next to him in the back seat of the car with James on my other side, the space felt much smaller than it actually was.

His hands were like blocks of knuckles at the ends of strong forearms. His fingers were so solid that I was amazed at their ability to manoeuvre tiny objects into tiny places — sim cards into phones, for example. A slight tremor was evident when he was undertaking such tasks, but it was never a cause for complaint. In fact, Adam was uncomplaining altogether. He was never sick. You could count the total number of his days off school on one hand.

Growing up, he didn't know his own strength for a while. As kids he, James and I would occasionally scuffle, which a couple of times resulted in Adam accidentally knocking my head against a table or James's against a heater. Another time I pinned a provocative note to the transom window above my bedroom door and he leaped up to hit the glass, shattering it onto me below. On such occasions, James and I were as responsible as he was for the damage. But, lacking cunning and slow to accuse, he was apologetic for us all.

Ad was a man who would let his hands hang by his sides when he talked to you. Sure, he had the tendency to rub his knuckles, and one hand was usually holding a beer. But there was no affected stance about him. He was a man who stood with his hands by his sides and his feet firmly on the floor. I don't think it occurred to him to stand any other way.

He could have been described as an introvert. He didn't seek attention or talk over others, nor was he demonstrative in his emotions or worries. But he was also gregarious and loved by friends for his crazy antics. He once sculled a bottle of chocolate sauce for a video camera and usually raised an eyebrow for photographs, mimicking his favourite wrestling star, The Rock. He had a raucous sense of humour and loved English comedy in particular. Sometimes he couldn't make it to the end of a joke he was telling as his blue eyes squeezed themselves closed and he laughed in a machine-gun patter. He had a loud, blokey voice and great ability to recite comedic scenes, as well as lyrics of songs in his favourite musical genres — heavy metal and gangster rap.

Adam was huge outside, but he was huge inside as well. His brow creased and furrowed as his mind wandered to daydreams or circumstances that remained a mystery to me. He had some obsessive-compulsive tendencies, making sure each car door was locked and checking on the front door a few times before leaving. For all his blokey-ness he was a loving and affectionate son, brother, boyfriend, friend. He'd pull us close for photographs, draping his arms over our shoulders so that his hands hung over us like big paws.

During his school years, Adam had witnessed some bullying and had perhaps even been the target of it himself. The bullies weren't the gargantuan lowlifes you see in cartoons, but self-entitled teasers who treated their peers with disdain. Adam was not a match for this kind of behaviour as slighting people did not come naturally to him. Perhaps as a result, he loathed arrogance and upstarts. Watching the news at night he would extend his middle finger at the television whenever these types of characters appeared, such as a teenager wearing yellow goggle-like sunglasses and a fur-trimmed hooded jacket boasting about his house party that cost the state thousands of dollars in a police response; or a unionist who played a lead role in ousting Kevin Rudd as the sitting prime minister. Ad's response was the same for these people and more — the bird at the screen until their faces were gone.

As he progressed through school it became evident that his strengths did not lie in academia. But from a young age, those strong, knuckly fingers would wrap around a pencil with finesse and work it with natural precision. He was a gifted artist, with the ability to replicate objects and images in front of him and the creativity to draw from his own imagination. When he graduated, Mum and Dad encouraged him to pursue something in the field of design. He did for a time, studying an apprenticeship in digital graphics, but was not enamoured with this chosen direction.

At times, Ad could be frustrating. If asked to take off his dirty shoes as he stepped through the door, he was likely to acknowledge the request and moments later proceed down the hallway with his shoes still on. But if Mum ever became exasperated with him, he would just hold out his arms and smile. 'Come 'ere,' he'd say before wrapping his bear-like arms around her. She'd look up at him and he'd look down, both of them laughing in their embrace. I think that my mother saw something of herself in her elder son's dreamy tendencies.

While he was studying he worked at a big, popular pub and was quickly drawn into the group of bouncers at the place — towering blokes who were older than him and who exerted quiet but powerful dominance over 'troublemaking pipsqueaks', as he'd call them. He had an innate sense of justice and was a proud and dutiful citizen. More than anything, he respected and admired police, the armed forces and those who were protectors and guardians in some way. Built like a workhorse and with a disposition more like the majestic, magnanimous Boxer in Orwell's *Animal Farm* than the cerebral and cynical pigs, Adam was made for security work with its protective ethos and long hours.

When he joined a security company that provided bouncers to pubs and clubs, he started working with a mountain of a man named Junior. Adam loved Junior's cheeky personality and how, with his stern face and commanding size, he would put the fear of God into any pub-goer he pleased. The first time Adam showed up for work — a white, blond guy, younger and smaller in build — Junior told him they had all thought Adam was the new boss. But Adam was one of them, and Junior, of Tongan background, called him a 'white brother' and 'Acama', Tongan for Adam. A few years older than Ad, Junior had his own wife and children to look after, and Ad came to regard him as an older brother. Junior was a God-fearing man who didn't allow swearing and wouldn't even touch Coca-Cola, teaching Adam not to touch the stuff either. Junior looked out for Ad, trained him in boxing, and Ad helped Junior move house and went to barbecues with his family.

Ad was happy enough doing security work, but he did not consider it his career. One day he was talking to Mum about seeing a few police cars nearby, and she saw how impressed he was by them. 'Do you want to be in the police force?' she asked, the thought only occurring to her as she spoke the words. His eyes lit up. But when he told Dad he wanted to join the police force, our father wasn't particularly enthusiastic.

I had always observed a deep love between my father and my elder brother. They were both strong, robust men who kissed and hugged each other at every greeting and farewell. Growing up, I'd regularly hear their voices coming from Ad's bedroom, long talks about how Ad was doing at school, whether he was achieving what he could and wanted, how he was helping around the house — all the things a father might try to bring out in his son. Dad and Ad had regularly had 'talks' — ever since Ad was young. Ad would always sit and listen to advice or criticism. If you had something to say to him, he'd always hear you out and respond graciously.

Dad understood Adam and worried that his twenty-three-year-old son's gentle personality wasn't suited to the police force, an environment of crooks, thugs and maybe bullying colleagues. But Ad insisted that it was what he wanted to do, so Dad did everything he could to help him get into the Bachelor of Justice Studies (Policing) at Charles Sturt University, which matriculated into the police training academy.

On 16 February 2004 Mum spent her and Chris's wedding anniversary with Adam in a sweltering motel room in Bathurst, ahead of the new university year. The Redfern riots were on the television and the town was dead quiet. Gail wondered whether police college had been a good idea. Adam told her that night that he wanted to be known by his first name, Chris. 'I hate the name "Adam",' he said. 'It's like a little boy's name.'

'Well, it's your life and your name,' she said. 'So you can do what you want.' The next day they drove to the orientation day at Charles Sturt University, where the air was cooler and a breeze blew through the green trees of the campus. Friendly faces and a festive atmosphere welcomed them. Adam approached the orientation desk.

'What's your name?' asked a senior student.

Adam and Mum looked at each other. 'Chris O'Brien,' he said and smiled at Mum. She knew then that this was the right place for him to be.

I had never seen my elder brother better than when he was studying at Charles Sturt in Bathurst and the Police Academy in Goulburn. He was healthy and fit from the physical training regime, relaxed from the country living and astute from the mental stimulation. He seemed to have found the right path in life and everything else was falling into place. Mum and Dad were proud and relieved.

Adam was finishing the second year of his degree when Dad was diagnosed with his brain tumour. He took the news hard, his protective nature helpless against this threat in his father's brain. In January 2007 he graduated from the Police Force Academy in Goulburn. The heat sizzled over the bitumen parade ground in country New South Wales and sweat dripped down the graduands' faces as they stood sharp and tall in long, straight rows, dressed in smart blue uniforms while their families watched from tiered seating. The O'Brien contingent was large, as nearly ten of us picked Adam out in the line and trained our eyes on him alone.

The ceremony ended and the newly minted officers let out a cheer as families and friends swarmed onto the parade ground. Dad stepped through the crowd tentatively, having recently undergone his first operation, searching for Ad among the sea of blue shirts. 'Addy!' he called. Ad heard and turned around. They walked towards each other and clasped in a long bear hug.

Mum and Dad had encouraged Adam to seek a placement at a police station in a country town. But he wanted to be where the action was and applied for five inner-city postings. He was stationed at Newtown Local Area Command and returned to live at home. His shift work created some free time during weekdays and he would often spend quiet afternoons with Dad.

Through the gap in the sliding doors to the sitting room where Dad often napped or read, I would see Ad sitting by Dad's stretched-out body, both talking quietly and solemnly. They often had these private conversations. I don't know exactly what they were about. I imagine that Dad was giving Ad advice, or a bit of a pep talk. They always seemed loving and tender.

Back in the rush of the city, the clarity and balance Ad had developed living in Bathurst and Goulburn seemed to diminish. His fitness routine waned and he drank more. The traffic caused him road rage. Most of all he worried for his father, and his anxiety about this translated into his work. He was not performing as well as he wished and decided to resign towards the end of his probationary year to focus on the family and himself. A short time later, Dad died.

Stoic and brave, Adam returned to his security work. He was living in an apartment in Drummoyne with his partner, Jaya, whom he planned to marry. He came to the house often and spent many hours sitting on the curved seat by Dad's ashes in the secret garden. Sometimes I would find him sitting in the living room with his brow furrowed and rubbing his knuckles, mulling things over in his mind.

Adam came to me one day and whispered, 'Hey, don't tell Mum, but ...' They were words I'd come to dread. Previous conversations that began with that phrase ended with me being made an unwilling accomplice in matters like tattoos, sky-diving ventures and a driving infringement.

He took off his T-shirt and turned around to show me his back. 'Look at this.' It was another tattoo. On his left shoulder was the inked image that I'd previously seen — a grotesque illustration of the scales of justice with skulls in place of the weighing dishes. Now he had a second tattoo covering his entire right shoulder. It was Dad's face, there on my brother's shoulder, smiling back at me, with a waving sash that sang 'Hero' flowing across it. Adam looked over his shoulder at me, smiling like a big kid. He seemed thoroughly satisfied with this means of displaying his adoration. 'Do you seriously plan to hide this from Mum?' I asked. He had already managed to hide the first tattoo from our parents, always wearing a surf shirt if he went swimming. He didn't plan for Mum to see this tattoo either, even though I'm sure he would have loved to show her.

He was working sixty-hour weeks as a security guard and seemed sleep-deprived. He would come over to our place on a Saturday afternoon after a busy morning with Jaya at Paddy's Markets or a Westfield shopping centre and collapse into a bed to have a nap. He wanted to get back into the police force or maybe even apply for the Australian Federal Police. He began examining his options and navigating the bureaucratic process and personal hurdles on his own.

He had to undergo surgery on his lower back for a very painful pilonidal cyst. Jaya, who was by this stage studying nursing, cared for him beautifully, dressing his post-surgical wound, which was more serious than Gail had anticipated. The wound didn't seem to be healing well, and Gail encouraged Adam to come back and live at home. But he wanted Jaya and himself to have their space.

He was protective of his widowed mother and when he stayed overnight would always make sure to kiss her goodbye in the morning, even if they had quarrelled or he had to leave for work before the sun was up. He would kiss her before he left without fail. If he didn't, he would get as far as the top of the driveway and have to turn around and come back down to the house to find her. One morning before leaving for work, he told her, 'Mum, it breaks my heart to see you sleeping in that bed alone.'

Then Adam suffered his first seizure.

Seizures

One night, about a year after Dad had died, Adam was in bed asleep when Jaya woke to find him having a fit. His rigid body was convulsing violently, his muscles were tense and his jaw clenched. She screamed and slapped him but he was unresponsive. She dialled Triple 0 and he was taken by ambulance to RPA.

When Gail arrived in the emergency ward, Adam was sitting up, smiling and chatting with Jaya, who told Gail that they were waiting for the results of a CT scan. James, Gareth and I arrived, and each hugged Adam tight. We couldn't understand what we were told had happened; he looked so well and healthy. We dragged chairs close to his bed, and drew the curtain around our area. The five of us huddled close within the tiny room with flowing walls we had made for ourselves. There was nothing to do but wait, and we took our cues from Adam, who was cheery, relaxed and cracking jokes.

'I'll give Dr Glen a call to tell him you won't be there for your appointment today,' Mum said. Dr Leslie Glen, a general surgeon, had operated on Adam's lower back and had known Chris and Gail for years.

Gail told him what had happened and Dr Glen expressed concern. 'Those tattoos are a cry for help,' he said.

'I'm sorry, did you say tattoos?' Gail asked.

Gail pulled aside the curtain and sat down. She was half-smiling as she said, 'Dr Glen said something about tattoos.' Adam's lips pursed as his eyes darted between James and me. Gail raised her eyebrows at her three guilty-looking children. We all laughed so loudly that from behind our blue curtain the other people in emergency must have wondered how people could be having such fun in such a place. Mum pulled aside the flimsy white gown and looked at the skulls of justice and then the image of Dad. 'Oh, Addy,' she said. 'We're going to get you all fixed up.'

Two specialists appeared at the curtain's entrance with images in their hands. The neurologist greeted Gail and swung the curtains back to make more room. James, Gareth and I left the bedside so that he could speak with Adam, Gail and Jaya. He told them that the CT scan revealed something — fluid on the frontal lobe. 'Why would that be there?' Gail asked, with some urgency. She had not expected them to find anything and was shocked to hear that they had.

'We can't say,' the neurologist said. 'It's probably been there a long time. It could either be congenital or from birth trauma.'

Gail was floored. The doctors explained that if the fluid was to be removed, Adam would need neurosurgery and a shunt. The prospect of Adam undergoing neurosurgery was incredible to us. So soon after all of those brain operations on Chris, Gail could not entertain the thought of her eldest son enduring the same. In any event, we understood that surgery was not a guaranteed solution. The stress Ad had been under — physical, emotional and work-related — could have contributed. He was working late nights and early mornings. He might have been drinking too much alcohol. The decision was made to wait and see if he had another seizure. He did. Over the next few months, Jaya woke up to the same scenario twice more.

Without a murmur of complaint or an ounce of self-pity, Adam attended appointments at the neurosciences department at RPA, and underwent electroencephalogram (EEG) testing to look at the electrical activity of his brain. He had to wear electrodes attached to his scalp with bandages wrapped around his head. They hung like snakes down his body and connected to a compact portable EEG recorder. He took a week off work to do the tests, but was told to wear the things as he carried out his normal daytime activities and during sleep. There had been months between the seizures, and between times he had seemed perfectly fine. So we weren't surprised when the test results, which didn't see a fit, were inconclusive.

What happened after this was a mystery to us all. Despite Gail's connections and knowledge of the medical system, it seemed as though we were falling through an enormous crack created by the inconclusive results. 'So what happens now?' they asked the neuroscience doctors. But there wasn't any clear answer.

Adam was so patient and undemanding. He'd spent months having tests done. He'd worn bandages on his head for a week. He and Jaya had travelled to Bali and Japan where he stood by a well with healing smoke billowing softly from it at a temple, scooping the smoke over his head, asking the curative powers to work on him. He continued to spend time in the garden where Dad's ashes were.

On 16 October, his twenty-ninth birthday, a strong windstorm engulfed Sydney, whipping up the Lane Cove River and bending the sprawling trees around our home. A single red helium balloon found its way across the rooftops and entwined its string around the azaleas surrounding the cross that stood above Chris's ashes. I found it and took a photo for Adam, who treasured and saved the red balloon. He and our mother heard the same message: 'Happy birthday, my darling son'.

Much more than James or me, Adam was interested in our mother's spiritual explorations. He accompanied her to Bowral to listen to a retired maxillofacial surgeon, Dr Tony Emmett, give a lecture about different levels of the consciousness. Dr Emmett and his wife, Annie, invited Gail and Adam to their home for lunch, where Tony told them about a woman, Joan Moysten, a friend of his with whom he'd travelled overseas. He described her as the most gifted intuitive he'd ever met. She lived in Strathfield, Tony said, and he recommended that they see her.

Adam wanted to go and meet this woman. He had asked Mum to take him to Suzy, but she had avoided this, fearing that anything Suzy said would become a self-fulfilling prophecy. Gail went to meet Joan on her own and their conversation was a philosophical one. At one point, Joan looked out the window and said 'everything you see out there is an illusion'.

'Well then, what is God?' Gail asked.

Joan took a blank piece of paper. 'See this? God is like this paper. And we are all playing out our lives on that.'

Even if Joan and Adam had nothing more than an interesting discussion, Gail thought Joan could be a good person for him to meet. They went to the Strathfield apartment block and sat in a bright corner of Joan's sitting room together. Joan talked generally for a time and Adam asked her some questions. Then their talk took an unexpected turn. Joan predicted a male death in our family in April. Adam and Mum looked at each other. April was two months away. Joan deflected. 'It could be a male animal.' Both their minds turned to our dog, Mr Menzies, who was by then fifteen years old.

They came home. Ad said to me, 'Hey, Jet, you'd better look after Mr Menzies okay because this woman said there'd be a male death in the family in April.'

'I *am* looking after him, I'm his twenty-four-hour nurse. I don't see you holding him up so he can take a piss.'

'All right, all right,' he said. 'I'm just telling you what she said.'

It was almost a year after Adam's first seizure and Adam and Jaya would frequently stay overnight, sleeping in our spare bedroom. At two o'clock one morning, Jaya ran into Gail's bedroom. 'Addy's fitting,' she said.

Adam was not conscious and his breathing was laboured. He was suffering a serious grand mal seizure, with violent muscle contractions, as well as arching his back and clenching his teeth. It appeared to ease off and he tried to stand up. At first Jaya and Gail thought he was regaining consciousness, but he came close to falling and they had to pull him back down onto the bed. This happened again and again for forty minutes or more: his big, strong body heaving itself up and the two women attempting to hold him on the bed. They were talking to him, but he was unresponsive. He urinated. It took a long time for him to become lucid again.

The next morning he was groggy but insisted that he had to go to work. James drove him in, and on the journey, told his brother he loved him.

Gail called her father and described what she'd seen. 'He needs to be on medication, Epilim or something,' he said.

Gail called RPA neurosciences and made an urgent appointment with a doctor Adam had seen before. She insisted that he be put on medication. 'Can't he be in the sleep clinic and you can see what's happening?'

'You can put him there if you want to, but I don't think that will show anything,' said the doctor. Gail was dumbfounded by this response, which she interpreted as nonchalance, and made the appointment at the sleep clinic herself. However, on the day of the scheduled appointment Adam was rostered to work a shift, so he phoned the clinic and changed it to a week or so later.

One Sunday in mid-April, Adam attended mass with Mum, which was unusual. Gail was very worried about her eldest son, who seemed so lost without his father. After mass they sat in the sunshine and talked about his future.

The following Thursday, Ad slept the night at home. He went in to Mum's room before six on the Friday morning — 29 April — to give her a kiss before work.

That day Gail looked at Mr Menzies. He was old and had Cushing's disease, was going blind and was unable to walk more than a few staggered steps. But he was loved and fed and seemed happy enough. He certainly didn't look as if he was about to drop dead the following day. 'That woman was wrong,' Gail said, bending down to scratch behind his ears.

While God is Marching On

On 30 April, a Saturday, Adam got out of bed early in the morning to wave Jaya off to work. They were then living with Jaya's mother in the western Sydney suburb of Greystanes. Jaya was working at an aged-care facility and rostered on the morning shift that day. They walked out to the front verandah together, where he kissed her goodbye. He returned to bed, alone.

The red balloon that the wind had brought on his birthday hovered in the corner of the room. Still inflated a half year later, it levitated as our dear angelic Adam slept.

Across the city, at home, Mum had woken up that morning feeling depressed, which was unlike her. She was unmotivated to get dressed and sat on the bedroom floor talking to her sister on the phone, which she normally would have regarded as wasting time. Meanwhile Jaya worked, James ate breakfast and I slept.

You'd think that you'd feel something, intuit it, if your beloved was drawing his last breath. But we felt nothing. We were oblivious.

Outside that small Greystanes house, not a noise was heard, as in that bedroom, alone, asleep, Adam's brain and body suffered a paroxysmal seizure and he crashed to the floor. The Epilim pills sat on the table beside his bed.

When Jaya arrived home in the early afternoon, she found him face down on the carpet. She rolled him over. She screamed his name in horror.

From his bedroom upstairs, James heard Mum's phone ring in the downstairs foyer. Her voice answered, and raised in volume. 'Give him mouth to mouth, give him mouth to mouth,' he heard her say. James squeaked the handle of his door around, pulled it open and peered over the landing banister. Gail was hanging up. 'James,' she called loudly, before seeing he was close to her. 'James, come with me, there's something wrong with Adam.' They ran to the car and scrambled in.

'What's wrong? What's happening?' James asked.

'Adam's turned blue and he's on the floor.'

They were stopped at traffic lights a few minutes from home, when Mum's phone rang again. Hooked into the car's bluetooth, Jaya's voice came across the car's speakers. 'The ambulance is here,' Jaya wept. 'Gail, Adam's deceased. He's died.'

James felt a physical sensation in his stomach, like he'd been kicked and winded. Mum stared straight ahead. Neither of them said anything. The seconds in this new world ticked by. The traffic light changed to green and cars in front moved forward. Gail automatically put her foot to the accelerator. 'We're on our way, Jaya. We'll be there shortly.' She pushed the red telephone symbol on the car's display to hang up. 'This can't be right.' They were silent for a moment, suspended in disbelief. 'Jaya can't be right.'

Past the Olympic site and onto the M4, Gail made her way westward to Greystanes. They arrived at a house cordoned off by police tape. A police officer said something about treating it as a crime scene. James ran in ahead and found his brother on the floor. Adam's face was blue from the blood that had pooled there. There was no mistaking that he was dead. James ran out of the bedroom. 'You can't go in there, Mum.'

Her eyes wide, Mum pushed past him. At the bedroom doorway she saw Adam. In that moment, she was stripped of everything. Who she was and all she had fell away at the sight of her son's lifeless body. Through the home stung the sound of our mother's scream.

'Mum, stop, stop!' James held out his arms. She hit her younger son's hand away and broke down by her older son's body. Her big, strong, angelic boy. Up she hauled her body and moved into the living room. She crouched down by a couch and sat on the floor.

James took her phone and started making calls. I didn't answer. James dialled Gareth instead, whose normally soft voice became harsh. 'What?' he asked in disbelief. Then James phoned Gail's sister Linda, Carmel, Mike O'Brien. He sat on the kerb outside the house and called his best friend, Will, and girlfriend, Lulu.

Back in Hunters Hill, I was up and dressed and had decided to take Mr Menzies for a walk. We had paused by a wall while Mr Menzies investigated its evidently wonderful scents. I smiled as I saw Gareth's car pull up. He got out and walked toward me, and his familiar face seemed changed. He told me Adam was dead. The ground rose up to meet my knees. Gareth picked up the dog and helped me get into the car. I lay down in the front seat as Gareth drove.

We arrived to find James and Mum with Jaya and Jaya's mother out the front. 'It'll be okay. It'll be okay,' I garbled as the three of us clasped each other. Linda, Carmel and Phil arrived. We waited outside the home as paramedics and police cleared the scene. A long white van pulled into the driveway.

Inside the bedroom, Adam was loaded onto a stretcher. The blood in his face had dispersed and he looked like our beautiful boy again. He could have been asleep. James was by his body, and Mum went to cut locks of his hair. She turned and held out her hand to me. 'Come on, sweetie.' But I couldn't move beyond the bridge of the door. I turned for the street and bent into the gutter, vomiting. When I looked up again, Adam had been packed into the van, which was pulling out of the driveway. It glided down the street, carrying him into the darkness.

At home, Gail sat in Chris's blue armchair as four nieces — her brother Murray's daughters — silently surrounded her. They were like angels with their big, sad eyes in beautiful faces and their soft touches. They did not speak, they simply encircled her, offering their compassion and strength with their silent presence. They'd done the same for me, when they'd found me sitting alone at Dad's wake.

Gail steeled herself. *We just need to get through this.* James stayed with her that night. It was the worst night she had endured. James couldn't sleep. He kept seeing the ghastly image of his brother's body. He got up and went to the bathroom. He staggered back, pawing his arms through the air, saying Adam's name. 'Ad, Ad,' he moaned, grasping at the invisible. Gail pulled him to bed. She had to help him sleep. She put on a meditation tape and stroked his back with her fingers. Up and down, with long, soothing strokes, the way he loved when he was a baby. Her arm ached as she held on and on through the night. Downstairs, I sat by Jaya on the couch, as she wailed for her Addy.

The next day passed but Gail did not make any calls. She did not tell anyone what had happened: the news would spread on its own. She and James sat in the morgue, as the coroner would have to determine the cause of death before Adam's body could be taken to a funeral parlour.

The morgue, in an old building in Camperdown, is less austere than one might expect. The kind staff led James and Gail into a small sitting room with comfortable chairs. Two closed doors adjoined the room and Adam was behind one of those. When they went in, he was wearing white and lying on a hard, silver bench. He was pale but looked perfect. There were his closed eyes, his soft lips, his button nose, his blond eyebrows, his rough stubble, his strong arms and knuckly hands. They kissed him, lay their heads on him. They would see him again, when they brought me and the rest of the family.

We learned that the cause of death might have been something called sudden unexpected death in epilepsy (SUDEP). Not much seems to be known about it, despite it being the leading cause of death in young adults with uncontrolled seizures. About one hundred and fifty young people die from SUDEP in Australia each year. An autopsy might have told us why Adam stopped breathing, but Gail refused to allow it. 'It's not going to bring him back,' she told me. 'What happened in that room? He had a massive, massive fit. His death was the consequence of that. We don't need to know if he stopped breathing because of this or that reason. I won't do it just to satisfy curiosity.'

Mum lay on the couch in the living room. The windows onto the garden were hidden behind heavy curtains. I'd never seen them drawn before. Sharp sunlight crept through the cracks. She opened her eyes as I entered. She bent her knees upwards to make room as I perched on the edge of the couch. She rested her wrists across her forehead. I leaned forward and placed my head in my hands. She stared up at the ceiling. I stared down at the floor. We were all arms, knees and silence. We did not speak. It turned out Mum couldn't. She'd lost her voice.

Here we were again. The four of us in the same little chapel at W.N. Bull Funerals. 'Death stalks tragic family' was the *Daily Telegraph* headline. The King Street traffic roared by outside and the raw sun streamed through the window. 'How dazzlingly the sunshine is flooding the hills around! It is like a mockery,' wrote Mark Twain after his daughter Jean died after an epileptic seizure in the bath.

Adam lay where Dad had been not two years before. He was dressed in his big security boots and pants. He wore one of his favourite T-shirts.

Here we were once more, surrounded by the friends and relatives who had buoyed us after losing Dad, making plans for the service. Eulogies, hymns, readings, prayers of the faithful, reflection music, photographs. We chose a memorial card that had an illustration of a young, fair man being embraced by an older one with dark features and hair.

Gail's voice had all but disappeared. On the day of the funeral she still couldn't speak. It seemed her emotional body had manifested a dramatic physical reaction with laryngitis that came out of nowhere.

His funeral took place on a Monday, nine days after his death. The same black cars, the same kind drivers from W.N. Bull. Hundreds of people crammed into our parish church Villa Maria to celebrate the life of a gentle, humble man. Though Adam had no longer been a police officer at the time of his death, former colleagues from Newtown LAC attended in uniform and formed a guard of honour. Police, security guards, school friends, doctors, businessmen, socialites, all came and cried for him.

Junior, Adam's close friend, had said: 'Mrs O'Brien, tell me it isn't true,' on the phone after he'd heard the news. Now he bent his huge body over the coffin and kissed it. He turned and looked down the aisle, staring beyond the doors of the church. His little boy bumped a tall candlestick, sending it falling towards the crowd. I heard gasps from behind me and cries of, 'Look out!' Junior extended his hand and caught the candlestick, not turning his head or changing his solemn expression.

Adam's closest friends wore the bright colourful T-shirts he had loved so much. They lifted the coffin onto their shoulders and carried him out — the grand rhythm of the 'Battle Hymn' ringing in our ears.

In the beauty of the lilies Christ was born across the sea,
With a glory in His bosom that transfigures you and me:
As He died to make men holy, let us die to make men free,
While God is marching on.
Glory, glory, hallelujah!

It was cold comfort to think that Adam probably wouldn't have known he was about to die. Part of me wished he had died in battle or working, fighting a bear or jumping over the side of a cruise ship to save someone. His death might have been of the kind that is glorified and declared honourable. A good death. It would have been worthy of a man so committed to protection and service. He wouldn't even have flinched at this. Instead, he was robbed. He fell asleep at the age of twenty-nine and never woke up. *What demented plan could this be a part of?* I asked myself as his coffin was loaded into the hearse. But I knew there was no plan. This was the cruel, random universe operating in all its grand indifference.

Here it was again. A beautiful cedar box filled with ashes. Would we bury these in the garden too? We couldn't bear to do it all again. Adam's ashes were placed in a pretty cupboard next to Gail's bed that had belonged to Dad and now held precious objects. Every time she opened that cupboard she could smell them. It was not a comforting smell. It was unfinished business. She knew that his ashes needed to be in the earth. He and his father needed to be together. But it would take three years to muster the strength to see it through.

E.M. Forster wrote that, 'One death may explain itself, but it throws no light upon another; the groping inquiry must begin anew.' The aftermath of Adam's death was very different from Dad's in many ways. There was no building named after Adam. No best-selling memoir. No radio interviews with his voice or newspaper clippings with his photographs. We just had the memories of him, having known him in all his ordinary, imperfect splendour.

Dad's death had come after a period of dread and expectation, while Adam's was a sudden shock. Contrary to what some people assume, one was not worse than the other. They each brought their own torments.

There was our grief, riddled with questions and guilt. Adam was gentler, quieter, more unassuming, more undemanding than Chris had been. Did we forget him? Did we let him down? He was the best, the truest of us all. Did we tell him that? Did he know how loved and adored he was?

And there was a new question too: how should you live your life now? My brother's life was as precious and valuable as my father's. What does it mean to have a good life?

And once again there was the loss. The terrible, maddening loss. Adam's entire life had been shorter than many people's after retiring age. He had been robbed. But who robbed him? Who robbed us?

When Dad was ill, I had prayed every night. But now I told Father Kev I couldn't. I had nothing to say. 'You could pray in silence,' he said. 'You don't have to say anything.' So that's what I did. I was silent towards God, as I felt God was towards me. And when I needed to speak into the void, all I could say was, 'Dad, you wouldn't believe what has happened.'

The Answer Lies Within

My mother kept her faith. She did not believe that Adam was with Dad; she knew it to be so. She did not harden. She appeared to fold her son and husband into her heart and continue up the mountain. Adam and Chris are ever-present with Gail, their lives, their illnesses, their deaths: from those days of heady bliss when she married Chris and gave birth to Adam to the horror of learning the news about them both and seeing what happened to them with her own eyes. Every moment remains with her. Every part of them rests in her. She bears all this, all of them, folding them within.

Some people would say that if the same happened to them, they could not survive, they would 'simply curl up and die'. But that's the thing. For better or worse, you don't.

Every night Gail lay herself down in bed as a guided meditation began to play. She hovered between waking and sleeping. She waited. Soon, eyes were looking at her from the darkness. Thousands and thousands of eyes.

The first time my mother heard the name of Jo Boney, a healing touch and spiritual practitioner working in a professional practice called Anam Cara Healing, she took little notice. The second time someone mentioned the name to her, she took notice. The third time, she knew she had to meet this woman. 'Did you just say Jo Boney?' Gail asked the friend who had been speaking. 'Would you give me her phone number please? I think I'm supposed to contact her.' Gail was familiar with the term Anam Cara as the title of a book by John O'Donohue. She was not familiar with healing touch therapy, which uses energy fields to heal.

Gail called Jo, who suggested they meet. When Gail walked into the beautiful room, heard the quiet music and smelled the sweet aroma, she knew that she was supposed to be there. Her decision to trust her instinct to call Jo was correct.

They sat and talked about what had brought Gail there until Jo asked, 'Do you want to try it, and see what I do?' Gail climbed up onto the massage table and lay down. Jo placed a soft blanket over her. Gail felt warm and comfortable. Jo stood on Gail's right, said a silent prayer and placed her hands on Gail's arm. Her hands moved to different parts of Gail's body, to her stomach, her neck. Then, gently, Jo put her hands on Gail's head. Instantly Gail saw a coursing river of light like shooting stars moving across her. The milky image of a hand waved through, as the light flew over and around her.

Jo continued to move her hands over Gail's body for an hour, and indicated that she'd finished by touching Gail on one arm. Gail didn't want the session to be over. She sat up. 'How do you feel?' Jo asked. Gail tried to speak and started crying, the most visceral outpouring of pent-up grief she had experienced.

By the time she left she had been there for three hours and paid the nominal fee. She made an appointment to go back the following week, and continued after that. The healing sessions did not always result in the same level of outpouring, but they were always very powerful. Gail attended these touch healing sessions for twelve months, and they gradually became gentle and calm. Rather than seeing coursing and shooting light, Gail progressively felt just a soft, floating glow around her.

She continued her walks through Kelly's Bush. She visited the magnificent fungus-covered tree trunks that, months before, she had thought had personal significance for her. There they were, those two beautiful trunks growing together out of the ground. *We are still two, together as one*, she had thought they meant. But now they seemed to represent her husband and son. She crouched down. She was weary, exhausted by all this searching and questioning. For months she had been coming, going, reading, listening, questioning, exploring, communing, contemplating, meditating on life and death.

Now, here, in familiar bushland near her home in Hunters Hill — not in Bhutan or Santa Fe or New Zealand or Alice Springs — she had a moment of clarity and insight: *Stop searching outside myself. The answers lie within me.* Suddenly, she knew. Finally, she could stop this frenetic searching and breathe. *There is a current in everyone's life. Stop rowing against it. Just lift the oars and flow downstream.*

My darling Juliette,

I am thankful that your father did not have to endure the sudden death of our beautiful Adam.

Enduring Chris's illness and death took nerves of steel, but the cry of the mother who has lost her child is primeval. Passed down through the ages, the cry of all mothers, through all worlds, through all time and space.

I was recently asked to give a speech on the topic 'resilience', which I found somewhat daunting! Did this mean that I was somehow regarded as resilient? Everyone has their own motivations and their own fears — what aphorisms can I say about resilience that will work for anyone else?

I do believe it is how we respond to events and situations that defines who we are and that WE, with choice and our free will, create our own reality, as we dance the rhythm of this moving world.

As I prepared for the speech, I asked your grandfather, who, as you know, I regard as the wisest man on the planet, what were his thoughts on resilience. I asked him if he thought it a process, or a personal trait?

He wasn't much help because his favourite book is the dictionary and he was keen to refer to that (which defined resilience as buoyancy, bouncing back as if spring loaded or in terms of health, recuperating, if you'd like to know). From that we discussed the importance of a happy childhood, loving parents and strong family ties, which I have been so fortunate to have had. In the end he gave up and just said in his broad Irish brogue, 'It's because you were born in little old Dublin!'

As I look at my wonderful parents and all that they have endured and overcome in their lives, I do believe I have a genetic predisposition to resilience as the second eldest of six children. We were loved, but not cosseted, and allowed to learn from our mistakes.

And if we look to the philosopher Carl Jung for answers, perhaps it is an inherited blueprint of experiences and responses which have been passed between individuals and across tribes and generations for hundreds of years which defines us as resilient. Or not. After all, we all just start out as one cell containing our specific genome which multiplies into the living, breathing, thinking organisms that we are. We are all around us and as individuals beset by crises of varying degrees of gravity. I am no different from anyone else.

In my own case, these traumatic and unexpected family events in close succession are a great deal to process by any measure.

I never thought I would be on the receiving end of people saying, 'I don't know what to say to you.' Certainly it is confronting when we try to place ourselves in another's shoes. We ask ourselves, 'How would I respond?' We doubt our own capacity to cope, to rise from the ashes. But I believe with strong grounding in love, hope, connection and purpose we are imminently adaptable and the human spirit will ultimately triumph over fear. What I do know factually is that different personality types will process a life event differently.

Now, I can genuinely say that I am deeply grateful for the opportunity to search more deeply for profound meaning. The process has not been one of contemplative philosophising. Rather, it has been a punishing journey of trying to grasp why this has happened and where our beloveds have gone.

When I looked at myself in the mirror as I was preparing for your father's state funeral, and said, 'I am not going to be a victim to this,' I was applying the mind-over-matter approach. But what I did not consider was the fact that this was not something that was perpetrated on me: it happened to your father.

On returning home in the evening with you, Adam and James after the funeral and wake, all of us drained and bereft despite having put on a courageous show all day, remember I assured you that Dad would not have left us. 'He loved us too much, and I'm going to find him,' I said.

So a search for truth, the enduring love of my son and husband — your brother and father — and an unquenchable desire and determination to see life for what it really is, has been a driving force these past years.

On a recent Saturday evening, I was at a Christmas party at Jonah's at Palm Beach. We were seated randomly but coincidentally I ended up sitting next to a couple who six weeks previously had lost their perfectly healthy thirty-two-year-old son suddenly from a heart arrhythmia. This was their first outing since the tragedy. We had never met before and they did not know my story.

With their son's recent death consuming every fibre of their beings, they started to tell me what had happened. Although it was early days they felt they had to get back into life. The mother of the young man told me that she would put on her mask to disguise the pain so others felt okay to talk to her.

We talked at length. I told her that it is not her responsibility to make others feel good or to feel obliged to get back into life as though nothing had happened. It takes time to find peace. To keep walking in the darkness, one foot in front of the other in a cumulative coping scenario.

Eventually noticing in small ways that strength is gradually returning.

In our Western culture where we are consumed with materialism and individualism we are polar opposite to the Eastern philosophy of community and spirituality. It is more acceptable to take days off work for physical illness than to grieve. We don't wear black armbands or dress in a way to tell people to be gentle with us.

I have learned that grief is not linear but cyclical. When you least expect it, there it is again. Our vulnerability and fragility can be cleverly disguised but they are never far from the surface.

Recognising the fragility of life brings me to a point of appreciation for each day rather than expectation. In so doing, the day is welcomed in and the story for the next brand new twenty-four hours starts to unfold. Tomorrow will have its own story.

You children roll your eyes when I remind you that it's about the journey, not the destination!

Descartes, the father of modern philosophy wrote 'Cogito Ergo Sum' ... 'I think therefore I am', his statement of what it means to be human. This brought me to my own realisation 'I think therefore I become' (not that I would dream of trying to compete with Descartes!). This realisation involves attitude which is intertwined with belief.

The following anecdote describes what I mean. I received a call two weeks ago from a friend who had also tragically lost her son and her husband a few years apart. I found myself disagreeing completely with her perception of our similar circumstances. She was desperate and asked me if I thought we had bad karma! Did we have some sort of cosmic debt to pay? I replied absolutely not, we had wonderful husbands and sons. How fortunate we were to have had them in our lives. The fact that their lifespans were not what we expected or wanted had nothing to do with us.

What happened to your father and Adam didn't happen to me: it happened to them! The depth of our pain is validation as to how much we loved, and were loved by, them. So that is good. That is what we want. To love and be loved on this earth.

Love, Mum

PART FOUR

This is Gail

The Main Event

Back in August 2009, six weeks after my dad died, I sat with Mum in the kitchen as she practised a speech she had been asked to deliver. She read from her pieces of paper in the same soft, sing-song tones she used for bedtime stories she read to us when we were small. 'I would like to thank Nat Zanardo, who has been a tireless supporter of the Head and Neck Cancer Institute,' she read aloud. She stopped and took a sip of water. I could see she was nervous. The plan had been for Chris to deliver a speech at this function. But after his death it made sense for Gail to step into his place.

My mother had never given a public speech before, except for her eulogy at Dad's funeral. Because I had been schooled during a time when public speaking was recognised as an important skill and probably impossible to avoid for an entire lifetime, I was able to offer practical tips — print the words in a large font, double space the lines, don't print into the bottom third of the page to stop your chin from dropping. Mum practised with me, reading the speech several times. When she finished, she put the papers down. 'I hope I won't be asked to do too many more of these,' she sighed.

But not long afterwards she was asked to open the Hunters Hill art show, and again spent a few hours preparing the short speech and practising it word for word. A few weeks after that, the deputy headmaster of Mulwaree High School in Goulburn asked whether she would speak at the school's speech night. Gail had to stop herself from asking, 'Me?' She was bemused and honoured but had no idea what she could say on such an occasion. She needed some moral support, which her younger sister Adrienne provided.

Adrienne and Gail look quite alike but their personalities are polar opposites. Adrienne, a loud and raucous nurse with a dry sense of humour and squawking laugh, chatted away as Gail's car cruised down the Hume Highway. They changed in a Goulburn motel room and found their way to the deputy headmaster's home for afternoon tea where they sat with their hosts in a pristine, old-fashioned living room. Mr and Mrs Wardle were warm and welcoming. They were very familiar with Chris's story, and it turned out that Mr Wardle had known him as a schoolboy. Their generous hospitality comforted Gail, although she couldn't shake her nervousness about her speech the following evening.

At the speech night ceremony a number of local dignitaries were present. Gail gave her talk, touching on Chris's life, work and her experiences. She told the students and their families about the tough lesson that life can change in a heartbeat. She wanted her speech to be inspiring for the young people and judging from the compliments she received, it must have been. But when one of the dignitaries described it as 'refreshing', it rattled her confidence.

At the end of the evening, the deputy headmaster and his wife escorted Gail and Adrienne to their car. They stood on the footpath, smiling and waving goodbye as Gail pulled away. Bang! Gail had backed into a school bin hidden from her view. Mr and Mrs Wardle bent down to look through the window and, flapping their hands, they shooed, 'Go! Go!' Gail and Adrienne made their getaway, leaving their accomplices behind in the dark night. The sisters soon descended into rolling, rollicking laughter. Gail hadn't laughed like that for months. It felt so good.

When she arrived home, Mum showed us the gift that Mulwaree High School had given her — a set of small wine glasses embossed with the school's crest in gold. I began to put them away into a cupboard in our kitchen. 'From now on, this will be the Cupboard of Awesomeness,' I decreed. 'Every time you do something awesome, Mum, we'll put the gift in here if you're given one.' As the speaking invitations rolled in, the Cupboard of Awesomeness filled up with gifts — pretty teacups and saucers, boxes of tea, more glasses and a small bottle of perfume. A beautiful Aboriginal carving from the kind folk in Narrandera in country New South Wales was put on a shelf for everyone to see.

In February 2010, Noelene (Chris and Gail's financial adviser) arranged for Gail to deliver the keynote address at the Genesys Wealth annual conference for financial advisers. Gail was to speak about their insurance arrangements and how our family had survived financially while Chris was ill and when he died. 'Not Taking Risk Insurance is Not Worth the Risk,' was the title of Gail's speech, referring to the insurance arrangements that Noelene had encouraged Gail and Chris to take and that meant we didn't have to sell our home after Chris died. This was the first time Gail had charged a speaking fee that, while modest, gave her hope that she might be able to derive an income from these speaking engagements.

I accompanied Mum to the conference in Auckland, New Zealand. I could see that it was a daunting exercise for her as she prepared a half-hour speech with audio-visual materials and practised it with me again and again. At the hotel, Gail took the lift down to the large auditorium to meet with the conference organisers and discuss her AV materials with the technical crew.

The conference MC, who was young and excessively confident, introduced himself. Making polite conversation while waiting for the sound check, Gail asked him how he came to do this gig. 'I'm a world champion public speaker,' he replied, quite seriously.

At the conference's plenary session I sat at the back of the dimmed auditorium to watch my mother talking to dozens of financial advisers. She wore a light-coloured dress that seemed to glow in the stage lights. Her talk included a video presentation that explained who Dad was. It showed his state funeral and included praise from Kevin Rudd and Charlie Teo. After that, there was an excerpt of a radio interview Chris had done on the ABC. As the video and audio played, Gail sat on a seat on the stage. I looked at her, neat and composed: she looked so small and lonely. But she did not feel alone. As Dad's face shone over her and his voice filled the room, she felt a cloak of protection around her.

The following night we lumbered into the conference's hired coaches and made small talk with attendees on our way to the conference dinner. On the third day, I knew Mum was relieved to have it all over and was looking forward to going home. It had been a depleting experience with a long lead-up period of preparation. At the conference's concluding session the world champion public speaker, a little less brash than he had been at first, presented her with a gift. Back in the hotel room she opened the small red box and pulled out a tiny glass kiwi. 'Now that's going straight to the Cupboard of Awesomeness,' I said.

The invitations to speak kept coming in. They were from schools, corporate events, fundraisers, retirement villages and countless Probus clubs. My mother forced herself to do these speeches, accepting every invitation possible. Chris had continued to accept these calls and appear at events until literally days before he died. It was clear that with his departure a gap had been created. My mother accepted the call for her to fill that gap — not to fulfil her own personal ambitions or drive, but to honour my father, to keep him alive.

At the same time she was finding her own voice. She was growing more comfortable with this role. She was embracing it. Her voice was gaining strength — literally — as she became more used to speaking to large groups. One evening, as I cooked dinner and she jotted down dot points for a speech the next day (for she no longer needed to write every speech out entirely), she made a remark partly to me, partly to herself, 'It's amazing how you develop at any age.' Life had taken a most feared and dreaded turn. But already, from the ashes, something new in my mother was rising.

Guarding the Vision

Heaven help those who take this on after Chris dies, Gail used to think as she observed the plans for Lifehouse taking shape in the final months of her husband's life. The task was enormous, and as colleagues came to see Chris, increasingly frail, in our home, it was as if he was about to take a long journey, and people were seeking as much as they could from him before he left.

My mother had not considered that she might be one of the people who would take on this responsibility. But about a month after Chris's funeral Bill Conley, the lawyer who had been at that first Sydney Head and Neck Cancer Institute meeting and who was now on the Lifehouse board, visited our home. He told Gail that the board had suggested that she should be invited to join. A few months later, the invitation arrived in a phone call from the chairman, Sam Chisholm.

Gail had met Sam Chisholm and his wife, Sue, on only a couple of occasions. The television businessman had the reputation of being a ruthless chief executive and managing director who had steered Kerry Packer's Nine Network and Murdoch's British Sky Broadcasting to media dominance with plenty of sackings along the way. Chris, a master at spotting an opportunity to make a useful ally, had approached Sam through Channel 9 contacts and persuaded him to be chairman. Sam had given Chris advice on the people who should make up the board.

On the phone, Sam was curt but genial. As well as inviting Gail onto the board he talked about the project's progress and hold-ups. 'I'm just going to get the building built,' he said. 'That's what I'm about.'

The following month, Gail attended her first board meeting in the sleek modern offices of the Deloitte consultancy firm. She had driven Chris there many times, negotiating the traffic-choked Victoria Road, illegally pulling up outside the building in the middle of Sydney's CBD to help her husband, who was unstable on his feet, out of the car.

On the first day that Gail was to attend the Deloitte offices for a board meeting without Chris, she took a very early ferry to make sure she was there on time. She knew all the board members personally but only a few of them well. The seventeen-strong board had only two women besides Gail, and two directors who were medically trained. They were an impressive group: intelligent, professionally successful and prominent in their fields.

Chris had handpicked these people as a pack mainly made up of heavy-hitting business and corporate animals who could drive the project forward. It would have been easy to feel intimidated. When she arrived, Guillaume Brahimi embraced her in a big hug, as did Paul Cave and Bill Conley. Everyone was warm and welcoming. She listened to the proceedings without contributing much. She didn't know what she could offer, but felt grateful to be there.

A few weeks later, Paul Cave and his wife, Carol, invited Gail to spend a weekend at their farmhouse in Berrima. It was one of the first trips she had taken without Chris. Driving the distance on her own and sleeping alone in a foreign bed might sound like unexceptional demands, but the most profound feelings of loss often lay in the everyday things. Gail drew comfort from Paul and Carol's tender friendship. She sat at their large wooden table on the sunny Sunday morning, drinking coffee and admiring the picture-perfect scene of black-and-white spotted cows in the distance and cumulus clouds in the sky.

The conversation turned to Lifehouse. Paul was genuinely enthusiastic in his praise of Gail's decision to join the board. He went on, however, to tell her he was concerned that, without Chris, there was a lack of clarity in certain aspects of the project. 'There is no vision statement,' he said. *What on earth is that?* Gail thought. She sensed that Paul had higher expectations of her than she had of herself. He seemed to believe that she could have an impact and could help to bring the vision to life. *What can I do about it?* she wondered. *Isn't everyone else an expert?*

As she drove home, the conversation preyed on her mind. She remembered Chris's words: *'I just don't want my name on a lemon.'* She had given her permission for this centre to bear his name. Now she realised that the name brought a duty. There was a risk that the thing might not live up to the man. The responsibility fell to her to ensure that the name and the vision went together. It fell to Gail to be Chris's voice.

Gail enlisted the help of her youngest sister, Linda, a former marketing executive and now in management with the Westfield corporation. The first thing Linda did was interview Gail, encouraging her to find order and reason in what Gail knew. I do not think my mother had realised the value of her own experience and knowledge of the project before this moment. She was not a professor or doctor, an administrator or health bureaucrat. She was Chris's wife, his carer, a highly intelligent, intuitive woman, manager of a busy surgical practice, cancer fundraiser and physiotherapist albeit non-practising for several years. She understood the complex issues of care and healing that Lifehouse was intended to address.

More than that, she had lived these issues. Our own experiences of a fragmented system of cancer care had seen us travelling from hospital to hospital for consultations with different doctors, multiple operations, blood tests, scans and chemotherapy. Mum would be fighting the traffic, searching and paying for parking, trying to manage Dad's nausea and headaches. She was always having to keep track of his illness and its history. She kept her own files. She and Dad were their own advocates. Nothing was easy. The chemotherapy agent had cost a fortune. The night following his third operation as she had closed the door to his room, she had felt so alone. All these things meant that she inherently knew the vision. 'The key is translating that to others,' Linda told her. Gail and Linda covered the dining-room walls with butcher's paper, onto which they wrote everything Gail knew. They used notes and emails on Chris's computer to trigger her memory.

'I need to speak with Andrew O'Connell,' Gail said as she came across emails between him and Chris. Andrew O'Connell is an Irish architect and creative talent who moved next door to us with his family soon after Chris's diagnosis. Chris and Andrew had many conversations about the Lifehouse building, which Chris had said many times should be more beautiful than clinical.

Andrew had recently travelled the world with senior university professors in a dedicated fact-finding trip to inspect top-tier universities and biomedical research facilities in the USA, UK and Australia. He had told Chris about his findings of the world's leading biomedical research facilities co-located on campus with the faculty of life sciences and close to large teaching hospitals. The key was the quality of the buildings, as Andrew explained, which encouraged the sharing of knowledge and facilities to drive successful research outcomes. These were not corporate or clinical buildings with fluorescent lights and cement walls. 'Buildings like that are more likely to make a person sick,' Andrew said. Rather, they were full of air and light, connected to the landscape, with warm colours. They were organised so that people would interact. Andrew demonstrated that there was a direct correlation between the quality of the facility and the outcomes produced from within it.

As Chris's health had deteriorated, he'd asked Andrew to meet with the recently appointed Lifehouse chief executive, Tim Dugan. Dad had known his time was running out. But when Gail saw Andrew, he explained to her that he had not been able to do this. 'I felt like I was letting Chris down,' he told her. 'But I didn't want to tell him I didn't have a forum,' meaning the opportunity to put this forward and be formally included.

Andrew looked at the current plans of the building and pointed to siloed spaces with individual clinics. 'Y'see, these don't encourage sharing and collaboration. It's all too sterile, too many white coats and orange signs screaming out "Clinic. Clinic. Clinic". It looks like a car showroom.' He pointed out the corporate colours, navy blue and orange. 'These aren't right. They're not conducive to a sense of wellbeing, healing, calm, peace.'

The final board meeting for the year was approaching and time was of the essence. The architects awarded tender would soon be announced and Gail was desperate for the built environment to represent the vision. If not, she believed Lifehouse was at risk of looking like a hospital not much different from any other.

With Linda and Andrew she collated a document that articulated the pillars of what Lifehouse should be. Andrew added images acquired from his trip that gave a sense of warmth, gentleness, safety. In the end they had on paper a hospital that would treat human beings, not just patients, where a holistic approach would help people feel at peace and full of hope. Private spaces for reflection and contemplation would be balanced with collaborative spaces for doctors and researchers. It would have a sense of place, be an inner sanctum enhanced by the quality of light, texture, natural materials, water, non-clinical spaces, zen garden spaces and feng shui. 'Imagine if Chris had been treated in a place like this,' Gail said. This place would be a testament to Chris's life and his work. But more than that — it would honour his suffering. It would harness the insights he discovered before he died.

Lessons in Politics

There was no time to waste: Gail felt that she needed to present the vision at the next board meeting to ensure the architects would be properly briefed. Linda suggested that she speak to Professor Michael Boyer, the director of the Sydney Cancer Centre and now Lifehouse, to enlist his support. 'You need to get his buy-in,' she said. This concept was a new one to Gail. The learning curve was steep as she absorbed the political strategising involved in board membership. Michael was very supportive and agreed that articulating the vision would be beneficial. He made many of his own contributions.

Gail had telephoned Sam on several occasions to discuss what she was putting together. He was guarded, but acquiescent. The night before the board meeting, Gail told him that she wanted Linda to present it and asked for permission for her sister to attend.

'I don't know what you want to do this for,' Sam said. 'Everyone knows what the vision is.'

'How do you see the vision, Sam?'

'It's a comprehensive cancer centre,' he snapped.

'And what do you understand that to mean?'

There was a pause.

'Sam,' Gail said, 'I felt concerned when you said to me, "I'm just going to get the building built." That doesn't instil much confidence that you understand the vision.'

Sam started shouting at Gail down the phone. Shocked, she pulled the receiver away from her ear. I went to the study door and could hear him from where I stood. Mum turned around to look at me. Her eyes were wide. She pressed the speaker-phone button, which sounded a click, and made his voice echo through the small, hard-surfaced room.

He stopped. 'Are you there?'

'Yes, I'm here, Sam.'

'Have you got me on speaker?'

'Yes, I have, Sam.'

Silence.

He calmed down and started to explain that sometimes he has a headmaster approach and gets the cane out. Gail's voice was steady. 'Just don't use the cane on me, Sam.'

The following morning, Gail met Linda outside the Deloitte offices and together they entered a particularly well attended board meeting with project managers, Lifehouse executives and others present with the board. When the agenda item came up, Gail introduced Linda with her CV, and explained that her sister would articulate the vision for Lifehouse. As Linda talked through the presentation, Gail observed the full room. She felt a surge of energy as she saw people becoming animated and excited. When Linda had finished speaking the project managers asked her for a copy of her presentation. Gail was ecstatic but also relieved. She felt that she had brought some clarity to the vision and could now leave it to those who knew best, trusting the people in that room to bring it to life.

'Does anyone have any questions?' Linda asked.

'Well,' said a voice from the other end of the table, 'I think that what this presentation has confirmed is that we're on the right track already.'

This was Gail's first inkling that she had trodden on some influential toes, that she had apparently invaded other people's territory.

Over the coming days and weeks she would repeatedly find herself faced with resistance from some members of the board and executive. During a holiday in Port Macquarie, her parents and sister Adele looked on incredulously as Gail struggled to get a word in during a telephone conversation in which someone remonstrated with her over the work she had done. My mother hates to talk on mobile phones at length because their link to brain cancer has not been ruled out, but she allowed the phone to get hot against her ear as she stood her ground.

I had never thought of my mother as someone who dealt with confrontation by meeting it head on. In fact, I don't think I had ever really seen her enter into a dispute before; Dad was usually the one who handled any dust-ups.

At first, I could see that she was uncomfortable with the situation. She would steel herself for phone calls, emails and meetings and take ages to recover from them, debriefing and replaying them over and over in her mind. But despite the emotional toll these confrontations took, she didn't back down.

She raised the issue of the logo, which had been changed after Chris died without any referral to her. It said in big bold letters, 'Lifehouse at RPA' and in small print underneath, 'the Chris O'Brien Cancer Centre' had replaced what previously said 'the new Sydney Cancer Centre'. 'The prime minister of Australia asked for my permission to name it The Chris O'Brien Cancer Centre,' she said to me again and again. 'Yet someone else has decided to turn his name into a tagline.' When Gail questioned it, she was flatly told, 'The logo is non-negotiable.' Later, a marketing executive would argue that the rationale was there would be more Lifehouse centres around Australia, carrying the names of other luminaries. Gail was furious. 'I'm not a marketing expert, but I would have thought that Chris O'Brien is the more powerful brand here, not Lifehouse,' Gail said to the woman.

There seemed to be a serious discrepancy between the sentiments Gail saw and heard in the community and those of the people entrusted to make Lifehouse a reality. At ground level, most people Gail spoke to seemed to know and love Chris. Some people even referred to Lifehouse as the 'Chris centre', and at speaking engagements she was regularly (and frustratingly) introduced as being from 'Lighthouse'. Meanwhile, the professionals at the nub of the organisation seemed blind to the value of Chris's name or Gail's contribution.

The months ticked by as Gail continued to fight for Chris's name and vision to be accepted as centrepieces rather than optional extras. This caused a great deal of tension between her and the executive team. In March 2010, she was sent an email essentially warning her not to step out of line. She was so enraged by this that she had to get out of bed and go for a walk at 1am. The next morning, she phoned Brian McCaughan, the colleague and good friend of Chris's who had told him that 'patients decide how long they will live'. A leading cardiothoracic surgeon and RPA man, Brian knew all about Lifehouse and had had many conversations with Chris about it. His advice to Gail was clear: 'If it were me, and I'm not telling you what to do, I would say that the situation is unacceptable and I'm considering my position on the board.' Gail took his advice, replying to everyone on the original email. Sam Chisholm quickly telephoned saying, 'I don't like to leave things swinging in the breeze.' He told her he wanted a meeting to discuss the vision and branding, and asked: 'Would "The Chris O'Brien Lifehouse at RPA" be acceptable to you?' Gail was satisfied (although later 'at RPA' was removed as the direct relationship between the two institutions changed). The meeting drew up a new branding style guide that was in line with the presentation Gail had produced. At the end, somebody stood up and said, 'I think you've been very brave, Gail.' Gail hadn't considered her actions to be brave. Why should she have to be brave to do what she had done? But the important thing was: mission accomplished.

It was also agreed that Gail should continue in her direction as the 'guardian of the vision'. But in the coming months she would repeatedly be reminded that the consent was limited. Guarding the vision meant that her interests seeped into every crevice of the organisation's development, from the design of the building to the staff members, their training, even the artworks hanging on the walls. She was out there in the community telling people that Chris O'Brien Lifehouse would be different from other cancer hospitals. Chris had told countless audiences that the Lifehouse would have integrative, holistic services available. Now she was out there telling people the same. But was she standing out on a ledge alone?

She continued to give speeches at dozens of community fundraisers, collecting cheques for anything from a few hundred dollars to tens of thousands. Elderly men and women passed around hats at Probus club meetings, people of all ages and means contributed. Gail couldn't turn a blind eye to the prospect of a cent being wasted. She knew what the community wanted because she heard the requests directly. She responded with loyalty because these were the people Chris had served.

The issue of protecting Chris's name continued to consume my mother. Uniforms appeared that simply said 'Lifehouse' and the website domain was nothing more than LH. 'Why can't it be COB Lifehouse?' Gail asked, and couldn't believe the response: 'Because people might get it confused with "Close of Business".' Gail recalled that Chris had spent his dying days toiling for Lifehouse and she was incensed that employees would tell her that her husband's name wasn't essential and should be dropped when it suited them. She persisted and tensions rose. 'Everything everyone says gets back to me,' Mum joked in a melodramatic tone one night. Thanks to a lifetime of friends and acquaintances throughout RPA, the Sydney Cancer Centre and the Chris O'Brien Lifehouse, it almost seemed to be true.

I have no doubt that people behaved differently towards my mother than they did towards my father. He had immense 'moral authority' in Tony Abbott's words, thanks to his professional credentials and personal circumstances. He also had a strong, commanding presence. Meanwhile my mother seems soft, feminine and even sweet. She has a lifetime of personal experience, but no specialist letters after her name.

My mother's drive to protect and uphold my father's name was formidable. Those big letters spelling 'Chris O'Brien' might not have been on the front of that glorious building today if it weren't for her. But it came at a cost. When she agreed to be on the board, she hadn't expected to take on such an active role, and when she did she hadn't expected to encounter such resistance. The more time that passed, the greater resistance she met. And the more resistance she met, the more determined she became.

The Deep End

I know that my mother would speak to my father during these months, asking him to help her, to guide her, to send her the people and answers she needed.

As she walked on her own and relished the solitude of Kelly's Bush one day, the silence was broken by the familiar warbling of a magpie. It settled close to her in a white gum. The bird and woman looked at each other for a while before the magpie took flight, circled her and settled on her other side. It seemed to follow her down the path and as she reached a clearing, it hovered about three metres above her head for several seconds before flying off and leaving her alone. Her lessons in spiritual direction had opened her eyes and she would not miss any sign or opportunity by dismissing it.

The architect produced magnificent designs for a beautiful built environment. Concerned that there would be too little money to realise the plans, Gail decided to pursue opportunities to raise more capital. She put herself in front of as many people of influence as she could. Any request to speak or advocate was a potential opening. She didn't believe in dead ends because, as she said, 'You don't know how the dots are going to connect.' Gail agreed to be the 'health ambassador' for Telstra's 'Ideas for Good' initiative, thinking it could lead to a relationship with the Telstra Foundation. Being asked seemed like an honour too. 'They could have asked anyone in the whole country to do this, but for some reason they chose me.' I watched as she did various promotional appearances on TV and radio for the initiative. She had to start writing a blog. It was all time-consuming — and unpaid — and after a few months, it became obvious that a quid pro quo wasn't part of the deal. She was already doing enough pro bono work for the Chris O'Brien Lifehouse; she didn't need to be doing it for a huge company as well. She must have said as much to Telstra, because a meeting was arranged with the foundation. It duly took place, but seemed inconclusive.

In May 2010 Gail was involved in publicity for Brain Tumour Awareness Week which resulted in her photograph being in the newspaper. The governor-general Quentin Bryce saw the image almost a year after she had presented Gail with Chris's posthumous Officer of the Order of Australia insignia. It had been a poignant ceremony in the grand reception room of Admiralty House. I remember that the room filled with laughter when the secretary of the orders, Stephen Brady, read an email he had received from Dad with some advice about facing a Senate estimates committee. 'Straight bat, protect your groin, let as many go through to the keeper as you can, feign exhaustion, memory loss or early dementia when really stuck. I will vouch for your incapacity to provide sane responses.'

After seeing Gail's photo in the paper, Quentin Bryce sent my mother an invitation to join her and Stephen for afternoon tea at Admiralty House. They greeted Gail warmly and after general conversation asked how Chris O'Brien Lifehouse was going. Prepared for this opportunity, Gail had taken the building plans with her. She showed them and talked about the progress. 'Gosh, Gail, this is a bit more than doing fundraising for the library at the local school,' Her Excellency said. She wanted to help, and suggested that she put Gail in touch with someone who might assist.

Andrew Forrest, the Western Australian miner who had recently been named the richest man in the country, could hardly have rejected the governor-general's suggestion that he meet with Gail. A date was set for the meeting at his apartment near the Opera House. In the preceding week, Gail told a senior Lifehouse executive her plans, but rather than being encouraging, he went red in the face and berated her for accepting. 'I need to be there,' he said. She replied that she had been given instructions to go on her own. 'If there's a second meeting you will certainly be included,' she added. He didn't seem mollified. The conversation turned to Telstra because it had been months since they had met with the foundation.

For the first time she heard that the Telstra Foundation wasn't interested in supporting them. Gail realised that nobody had bothered to let her know, despite the fact that she was still working as their Ideas for Good ambassador. 'I'll tell you what to do with Telstra—' he started to say, but Gail cut him off. 'I don't need *you* to tell me what to do with Telstra.'

Gail was fed up. All the time and energy she was putting into Chris O'Brien Lifehouse was costing her financially as well as emotionally. She was not earning a salary, nor had she any stable income to speak of, yet her time was consumed by speeches, presentations, meetings, conversations, emails and other tasks. I was encouraging her to take a step back, telling her that Dad would never have wanted her to be in this stressful position. But one objective was driving her: to do her best to make sure that the Chris O'Brien Lifehouse lived up to her husband's name.

A few days later Gail took a ferry to Circular Quay to meet Andrew Forrest. She had no idea how she would be received. She was worried that he must be thinking, *What the hell is this woman coming to me for? Money, of course. What else?*

Gail was shown upstairs by the concierge and Andrew himself opened the door. He was younger than she'd expected and greeted her without any apparent suspiciousness. There was a vibrant energy about him that she recognised, and she relaxed immediately. Though she started her spiel about the hospital and its history, the conversation took a different turn. Gail was missing Chris so badly, and she was feeling battered by some of the people who were supposed to be bringing his vision to life. As she talked with this kind and receptive person, she succumbed to the angst and tension that had been building inside. She became emotional. Andrew pulled out a perfectly ironed handkerchief and told her to keep it. The meeting went longer than expected and he was due at a forum where he was giving the main address. His parents-in-law arrived at the apartment ready to go to the event; they looked at Gail quizzically as he asked them to wait in another room while they finished.

While this was happening, I was keeping an eye on the clock. As Mum's sounding board at nearly every step along the way, I was waiting for the right time to call her and ask how it went. When I rang, she had retreated to a nearby café for a solitary hot chocolate. 'It didn't go as expected,' she told me.

'What happened?' I asked.

'I cried,' said Gail.

'Oh, my God.' I was appalled and couldn't hide it. But as Mum described the meeting I could see that she hadn't embarrassed herself at all. After everything that had happened, she was unafraid to be real. It was not a weakness; it was her strength. Gail's conversations — and now friendship — with Andrew Forrest continue to this day.

Throughout this period, the number of community talks my mother was giving increased to as many as several each week — a plethora of Probus club meetings all around Sydney, Rotary, schools, fundraisers. Events might have been local or regional as she travelled to the Shoalhaven region, Narrandera, Mudgee, Dubbo, Milton, Young and many other towns in country New South Wales. It didn't matter whether the meetings were large or small. In Dubbo she went to the Stock and Stations ball, where the MC announced that as a fundraiser men could pay $50 for a dance with her.

By the end of 2010, Gail told her sister Linda that she was exhausted from it all. 'But it's so important, Gail, that you keep Chris's name alive,' said Linda. She suggested that at the next board meeting Gail should present her diary throughout the year and use that to request some support. She should emphasise that there was a hunger for Chris's story and his values in the community, a feeling that should be capitalised on. Gail collated her diary, consisting of hundreds of engagements. When the board papers arrived in the post and she checked the agenda, she saw that her item was last. She considered this placement indicative of their level of interest, so as soon as the meeting opened Gail interrupted Sam. 'Excuse me, chairman, I'd like my item to be brought forward to number three please.' Some people looked slightly shocked. Sam huffed and grumbled something about seeing what happened, but did call on her soon after.

Linda suggested that Gail meet a friend and colleague, Karen Bristow, who worked in public relations and could help her to prepare speeches, arrange logistics and give advice. After meeting the woman Gail steeled herself to ring Sam and suggest that Karen be brought on in a paid capacity to assist her. She never knew how he would react to her suggestions, but in this case he was receptive and invited both women for a meeting at his home. Here, Gail saw Sam in a different light for the first time. He obviously loved his wife, Sue, and his dog, Wilson, a giant schnauzer. Karen, a talkative country girl who gets on with everybody, won Sam over quickly and he agreed that she should work with Gail. With Karen's help, the work became enjoyable and manageable. As a director Gail was told she still could not be paid, but Karen was, giving their work together an acknowledgment of value.

When the NSW Liberal Party took office as the state government in 2011, Gail was told that the chief executive, Tim Dugan, and Lifehouse board member Max Moore Wilton had a meeting with the new state premier, Barry O'Farrell. The former secretary of John Howard's Department of Prime Minister and Cabinet and the chairman of many boards, Max was known as a tough administrator. Gail telephoned him and suggested that she attend the meeting too. He agreed that it might be helpful and the three attended together. The meeting was a positive one and indicated that Chris O'Brien Lifehouse had this new government's support. At the end, the then treasurer Mike Baird motioned out the window and said to Gail. 'I think Chris is happy.' She craned her neck. A vibrant rainbow against the dark sky filled her eyes. She turned back to the treasurer, who was mirroring her smile. 'Yes, he does that, you know,' she said.

There were times when Gail and Sam Chisholm continued to clash, and her relationships with other board members continued to have their troublesome moments.

Six weeks after Adam died, Gail was determined to attend the final board meeting of the financial year, despite her trauma. She had spent weeks working on a fundraising proposal and had been waiting for the opportunity to present it to the directors. Again, it was clear to her that she was seen to be overstepping the mark. The chairman had acquiesced and put it on the upcoming board meeting's agenda but when the day came, Sam grunted hello and a senior executive did not look her in the eye. Even though everybody had attended Adam's funeral weeks earlier and been sorry and supportive, their compassion did not necessarily extend to the boardroom.

Gail could tolerate it no longer. That night she wrote a long email that was her strongest protest against the treatment she had received. She condemned the behaviour she had encountered not just that day, but for the previous two years. 'The Chris O'Brien Lifehouse is supposed to look after people exactly like myself — it is supposed to mirror a kind, caring, compassionate culture,' she wrote. Yet they couldn't even show it to one of their own.

James and I were looking over Mum's shoulder at the computer as she finished writing. 'Shall I press send?' she asked.

'Yes, do it!' we said.

The next day, Mum went out. The home phone rang several times, and I eventually answered it.

'Sam Chisholm here, is your mother there?'

'No she's not.'

'When do you think she'll be home?'

'Sam, to be honest, I don't think she wants to speak to you.'
I told him that I thought that he and certain members of the
executive had treated my mother appallingly. We talked for forty-
five minutes — something I would never have considered doing
before Adam died, having felt deferential to Sam. But I was starting
to understand how my mother had shaken off caring about things
like overstepping her boundaries or what people thought.

'Did anyone even acknowledge my brother's death at the
board meeting?' I asked. To my surprise, Sam was receptive to
my forthrightness. He listened to everything I said and talked to
me as an equal.

I told Mum all of this when she arrived home. The next
day, Sam Chisholm rang again several times. 'I still don't want
to speak to him,' she said, but eventually she answered.

'Well, I got this email—' he started saying, but Gail quickly
leapt in.

'I'm not going to start explaining myself to you, Sam.'

'All right. Now, let's talk about this.'

Gail told him everything she thought and felt, all of the
moments of anguish and insult that she'd encountered. She was
bowling fast balls at him more strongly than she ever would
have expected. He received everything with his trademark
curtness but always invited a solution and encouraged all she

had to say. After an hour and a half he said, 'If you've been made to feel like that, well, I apologise.'

'I forgive you, Sam,' Gail said, feeling exhausted.

'I don't need forgiveness,' he retorted.

'Isn't that what we're all here for, Sam? Love and forgiveness?'

'All right then, let's profess undying love for one another, and get on with it.'

From that moment on, Sam Chisholm was regarded with some fondness in the O'Brien home. He was a bull in a china shop, but he had courage and refused to 'leave things swinging in the breeze'. Over the years Gail would see the softer sides of not only Sam, but many of the people and personalities she had come to know. The process had been painful, yet she had learned so much about herself and others, about human frailties, relationships and ego.

Bob McMillan became particularly close to my mother. A knockaround bloke who described himself as 'just a printer', Bob was a businessman who sold his large printing company for a fortune, and a friend of Chris's and powerful supporter of the SHNCI, the Sydney Cancer Centre and Chris O'Brien Lifehouse. Chris had met Bob when he drove to the hospital one Saturday to check on a patient and arrived cursing the owner of a huge Bentley that was parked across three spaces after he had been forced to circle the car park. 'Sorry I couldn't get here sooner,' he said to his patient. 'Some clown in a Bentley is taking up three spaces.'

'That'd be me,' came a jocular voice from the corner. It was Bob McMillan, who was visiting the same man.

Gail saw that when Bob became mad or frustrated it could be a case of 'He's gonna blow!' but she witnessed equally tender moments: he wiped tears from his cheeks as he walked his daughter down the aisle and trailed after his family with food and drink in his car as they rode in a 200-kilometre bicycle ride fundraiser. Some nights I would arrive home at night to find Mum sitting on the couch talking animatedly to Bob on the phone. Her heels would be propped up on the coffee table next to a glass of wine, just as Dad used to do. 'Bob's my mate now,' she'd say, hanging up the phone.

Max Moore Wilton was regarded as the toughest in the business world and Gail had felt quite intimidated by him in her first few months on the board. But as time went on, she came to know him as the most generous and reverent ally. In meetings, he would turn to her whenever he'd refer to 'Chris O'Brien'. He had tears in his eyes when he and his wife, Jan, approached our car at Adam's funeral and Jan reached through the window to hold my cheeks, saying, 'You poor little thing, you poor little thing.' Again Gail saw Max's emotions as he made a large donation on behalf of his wife and himself.

Gail had seen that Robin Crawford, a founding director of Macquarie Bank, had the potential to cut people down quickly with his sharp tongue. At times, she would wait with trepidation for his response. But she came to know a person with a great capacity for humility. As the previous chairman when Chris was still alive, Robin would come to our home to meet with him and whisper to us, 'I've come for my boxing around the ears.'

When Sam Chisholm resigned as chairman in 2012, he let his tough facade down entirely. 'You're an incredible woman, Gail. You've had to put up with all this rubbish from people,' he said. 'And with Chris and your son ...'

'Sam,' Gail said, 'that's the nicest thing you've ever said to me!'

'Well, don't tell anyone.'

Sweetie,

As I read back over all of this, I'm amazed that I had the gall to do all this, that I was so driven for the Chris O'Brien Lifehouse to succeed. Some people must have really wondered about this woman arriving at their offices, asking for their support.

I was so nervous when I went to see Nathan Rees very early on. My gosh, I've come such a long way since then. Rarely am I nervous now.

Plenty of people ignored me! But I don't even care about that any more. That's their way of saying no.

I am grateful for the passion, for I never would have had the motivation or the courage to do the things I have done, meet the people I have met, had the arguments that were necessary.

I have learned through all of this that I cannot force anything. I was just trying so hard, trying to force it to happen. Now I know that anything I try to force doesn't work. I have learned to trust. Trust is all about allowing life to bring you what it's meant to.

I have a contemplative practice every morning and evening. It is as routine as brushing my teeth. The most important part of this practice is gratitude and surrendering the day to spirit.

Sometimes I go down a track thinking it's for one reason, only to find out it's for another. Inevitably a connection made earlier comes around again in a different way, not what I expected. Again not in my control. If I don't act on it, the universe sends it again and again. We call these coincidences. I am wiser now. They are not coincidence.

Love, Mum

Back to Physiotherapy

In April 2012, almost three years after my father's death, my mother dreamed that she and he were sailing in the ocean and the boat began to sink. She kept diving down trying to pull the boat to the surface. My father was treading water and not helping her at all. He seemed quite calm. In the end she knew she had to just allow the boat to sink. There was no way she could pull it to the surface on her own. She awoke terribly upset. The dream disturbed her immensely. She realised that she had to stop trying to keep Chris alive. She had to stop organising her life around her attachment to him. 'I have to be me. I have to be Gail.'

She stood in front of her dressing table and took off her wedding ring still on her left hand's wedding finger. She hung it on a chain, never again to be worn on her finger.

Apart from fees from a handful of paid speaking engagements, Gail still had no real income. She needed to find a job, not just for money, but for her own sanity. She wanted to wake up in the morning and have structure in her life, to know that her work was valued because of the dollars in her bank account.

Throughout all the years that she didn't formally practise as a physiotherapist, Gail never gave up her registration and the continuing education to maintain it.

One early morning as she was entering Kelly's Bush, she held her chest and pleaded, 'Christie, please help me find a job.'

Not long afterwards Adam's partner, Jaya, feeling depressed about Adam, went into the tearoom at the care facility where she worked as a nurse. Rose Boulos, a physiotherapist, walked in to find her in tears. Jaya explained that her partner had died of an epileptic fit. Rose said, 'That's what Professor Chris O'Brien's son died from.'

'That's who he was,' said Jaya. 'Chris O'Brien's son.'

Rose sat down at the table and talked to Jaya for two hours. During the course of the conversation Jaya told her that Gail wanted to get back into physiotherapy. Rose said she wanted to help and gave Jaya her phone number to pass on to Gail.

Gail phoned Rose and they arranged to meet at an aged-care facility in inner-western Sydney. They sat in the sunshine for some time talking about Chris, Adam, life and death. Rose had actually attended Chris's state funeral. She said Gail would be perfect working in the company in which she was a supervising physiotherapist. It was called Vivir — Spanish for 'to live' — and supplied health services to aged-care facilities.

Gail's prayer had been answered. She was hired to work part-time at a beautifully appointed new facility in Rose Bay called Beresford Hall.

Not only had Gail retained her skills and knowledge, but she now had qualities that she could not have learned at the NSW College of Paramedical Studies all those years before. She brought wisdom, compassion and tenderness to her role as a physiotherapist. These made her a favourite among patients. One was Martin Eissenberg, a builder crippled with Parkinson's disease. Gail would take him down to the gym, get him on an exercise bike and make him walk in the parallel bars. It was such an effort, and was never going to rehabilitate him, but he loved it and Gail liked spending the time with him. I was once on the phone to my mother when Martin shuffled past her in the hall. 'I'll come to your room shortly and give you a massage, Mr Eissenberg,' she said. He didn't hear and she repeated herself.

'Oh, I'd love it if you would,' I heard his German accent say loud and clear, as he had moved very close to her and the receiver.

There was Iris, who must have once been very beautiful. She had written a book about her life. She had no children but was loved by nephews and nieces. Her lower legs were so swollen that Gail would remove her pressure stockings and massage the fluid-engorged limbs. One day some of her glamorous friends arrived and, thinking Gail was the beautician giving her a pedicure, they tried to book themselves in.

Then there was Stephen, only in his forties and suffering from the same brain tumour as my father. Stephen languished in that nursing home for months, making Gail see another fate that her husband could have suffered.

Gail spent a lot of time with Stephen as she mobilised his limbs and got him out of bed. He was very heavy but sometimes she managed to get him standing by the bar, like a ballet barre, in the hall. They spent a lot of time talking. He was very fond of Paulo Coelho's book *The Alchemist*, and had stuck a quote on his wardrobe that read: 'If something happens once it is unlikely to happen again, but if it happens twice it most certainly will happen a third time.' Stephen and Gail had long conversations that traversed many topics, but especially life and death. At one point, Stephen — a gay man — looked at her and said, 'I love you, Gail.'

Gail worked with Vivir for a year. She loved working with people and genuinely helping them, especially as she could see the immediate effects of her work. It felt good to be appreciated, too. She could heal herself through service to others, she believed. What's more, she seemed to be able to offer the patients something different from the other staff.

Then she was offered a casual job at Hunters Hill Private Hospital. It was convenient being close to home and she worked in the rehabilitation gym and hydrotherapy pool of a very busy orthopaedic environment. There was no time at all to think about her life outside those walls. That was healing in itself. Work became a release.

Gail persisted in her work for Chris O'Brien Lifehouse. After one meeting with chief information officers of other hospitals, Gail excused herself to go to her shift. She went into the bathroom and changed into her uniform, a red polo shirt and black pants, and returned to the table to say goodbye before she left. She learned later that the table had been surprised to see her emerge in a work uniform, realising only then that she had a day job besides Chris O'Brien Lifehouse.

Some patients at the hospital have said to Gail quietly, 'I know who you are,' and gone on to talk fondly about Chris. Recently, she was kneeling on the floor in front of a man and working on his knee which had recently undergone a replacement, when he bent down to her and said, 'I nominated you for Australian of the Year.' Gail didn't hear him at first and asked him to repeat what he'd said. She was so surprised and delighted, that she responded, 'Just for that, I'm going to give you an extra massage!'

In 2012, we were still surrounded by my father's possessions, and my brother's things had found their way home too. Although these physical traces had taken on an almost sacred form, my mother felt that it was time to let go.

One day, before leaving the house to attend a meeting at Chris O'Brien Lifehouse, Gail carried Chris's surfboard up the driveway. Chris hadn't been a particularly enthusiastic surfer but would always take his old board to Whale Beach on our holidays. Gail would spot him among the handful of surfers as she looked from the window of our small flat onto the beach's northern end. Now she propped the surfboard against the large camphor laurel tree on the nature strip and drove away looking at it in the rear-view mirror, watching as it became smaller and smaller in the distance.

When she arrived at the meeting at a café in Camperdown, she felt the deep well of sadness inside her that had been stirred. The purpose of the meeting was for her to introduce Petrea King to two operations employees at Chris O'Brien Lifehouse. Gail had been focused on her quest to ensure that the right people were advising and working at Chris O'Brien Lifehouse to help build a world-class integrative medicine or wellbeing centre. Through this, she had developed a relationship with Petrea, the well-known founder of the Quest for Life Centre in southern NSW and widely respected expert on matters of health and healing. Gail began to tell the group about the surfboard and became emotional. She had never cried in front of anyone at Chris O'Brien Lifehouse. But on this day a tear escaped as she described leaving it on the street, this tangible item from happy days gone by.

The employees seemed embarrassed. 'Look on the bright side,' one said, 'someone will come along who really needs a surfboard and they'll think this is great. You should feel good about that.' Gail knew that this person had simply been trying to fill an awkward moment. They weren't to know that nothing needed to be said; simply being present to her grief was enough. Later, when they were alone, Petrea touched Gail's arm. 'It doesn't hurt them to see your tears,' she said.

As time passed, my mother found it easier to part with clothing and items that she or I knew others would find useful. She collected all Dad's lovely shirts — washed, ironed, hanging on hangers and protected with plastic. My uncle Mike, Dad's brother, had told her he could store them in the spare room of his house, reassuring her that this was not breaking any bond or letting anything go. 'I am just storing them for you,' he said. 'I'm storing them at my home. Occasionally I might borrow one. I will make sure to wash it and return it.' Mike still has the shirts. My mother feels calm knowing they are with him. Now she is pleased when she sees one of her brothers or brothers-in-law wearing Chris's coats or jackets.

After Adam died, Gail was invited to a fundraiser for bereaved children. She placed a bid of $100 in the silent auction for a voucher with a business called Organise For Life. She won. 'It seems everyone else's life is completely organised,' she remarked to me back at home. A gentle woman named Angela Hunter, who had donated the item, introduced herself to Gail and came to the house. Together she and Gail worked their way through hundreds of items that had belonged to Chris and Adam. As efficiently as Mary Poppins but also sympathetically and delicately, Angela helped Gail to part with the unnecessary physical reminders that were ultimately burdensome. There were tears in the process, but Angela would gently suggest that Gail take a photo of the item, reminding Gail that the item itself was of no use to her but it might be to someone else. My mother was grateful for her empathy and kindness. Each time Angela left with a carload of things, Gail felt the burden lighten.

Of course, my mother was not only dealing with her own wellbeing — she was worried about my brother and me too.

After our elder brother's death, James, then twenty-one years old, struggled on through his Arts degree but floundered as he searched for purpose and direction. He had a beautiful, warm girlfriend, Lulu, and close friends who supported him throughout. Mum worried that his atheistic beliefs made recovery and healing more difficult. But eventually, he found his emotional equilibrium through worldly and wonderful things: a motorbike and a rescue Staffie named Jericho. Mum encouraged him to study a Music degree, which gave his talents an outlet, introduced him to kindred people and nourished his soul through daily creative energy and purpose.

Then twenty-seven, I had finally finished my Law degree and completed several unpaid legal internships while continuing to work for Fairfax Media. But otherwise I was increasingly a homebody who needed more and more sleep. I was lethargic, thin and emotionally volatile with a pallid complexion. I attended counselling and was prescribed anti-depressants but Mum thought that a more holistic look at my wellness was required. She organised for me to see Professor Kerryn Phelps, who was immensely thorough in checking my state of health with full blood counts and a referral to a nutritionist. As it turned out the blood tests revealed slightly irregular thyroid activity. As I sat across from Professor Phelps at her Surry Hills clinic, a shaft of light came through the window over her shoulder and hit the right side of my neck. Professor Phelps cocked her head to the side, 'I think you have a lump there.' She felt my neck and, indeed, the light had revealed the shadow of a lump. Professor Phelps referred me to pathology at the Mater Hospital to have a fine-needle biopsy of my thyroid gland. When the clinic telephoned to say the results had arrived, the receptionist said, 'Professor Phelps has asked you to bring your mother to the appointment.' Mum and I sat in Professor Phelps's office as she told us that the biopsy confirmed a thyroid carcinoma. I looked at my mother. Her eyes were glassy and her lips thin. She said something about the Biblical book of Job, and being tested. 'This has to be caused by immense emotional stress,' she said.

'It's a good prognosis,' Professor Phelps assured us and we both sighed our relief. I understood that I had been set on a course that we would travel slowly and purposefully. Papillary thyroid carcinoma, I would learn, is a non-aggressive albeit malignant cancer that has an exceptionally high cure rate for small lesions in young patients.

Professor Phelps had researched the best surgeons in the field, but we knew who they were already — Dad's head and neck surgical colleagues. 'We'll call Anthony Clifford,' Mum said, and recited his office telephone number to Kerryn by heart: it was the same number as Dad's as they had shared rooms.

Even though I do not have the same faith as my mother, I don't mind telling this story as it is. That's simply what happened — light came through a window, fell on my neck, and Kerryn Phelps was alerted to a lump that otherwise would have gone undetected, at least in the short term. There's no doubt in our minds that Professor Phelps, the consummately thorough professional, would have detected the lump eventually without the help of happenstance. But it's a good story, nonetheless. And it's certainly one my mother deeply appreciates.

Today, having undergone surgery performed by Dr Clifford, the scar across my neck is barely visible. I remain under the excellent care of endocrinologist Dr Anne Maree Kean and the Nuclear Medicine department at RPA for monitoring purposes.

The Ashes

The rain fell hard at the burial of my father's mother in 1995 in the town of Wentworth Falls in the Blue Mountains west of Sydney. Rapids formed as it poured into the cemetery while our family stood and watched men heave with effort to lower the casket into the sodden earth. The drama gave the feeling that even nature paid homage to our loss.

By contrast, a crematorium lacks the atmosphere of a gravesite. There is no image and sound of effort as the body and coffin are lowered but rather a flimsy curtain inches a few metres across to hide the casket from view, making a pathetic little whirring sound as it goes. The finality of this moment is lost (evidenced by James sneaking behind the curtain anyway to have one last moment with his father's body).

For several reasons cremations are increasingly chosen instead of burials. They do seem to provide a neater option. But we learned that is the case only if the ashes have a place to rest.

My brother's ashes were in the small cupboard in my mother's room for more than three years. The cupboard was a special one, full of precious objects and memories. But it was wrong to keep them there. My mother felt that every time she opened it. Making a decision about where to place them was difficult. Not everybody has such an affiliation with the sea that they can be dropped in the ocean. So no decision became our decision.

On top of that, Gail's mind had been going in circles about whether to sell our house. The possibility of doing this prompted her to have Chris's ashes exhumed after lying in the garden for more than four years. Gail asked the gardener to bring them up. He did so, reverently and quietly, and let her know that he had placed them under the little stone seat. They too sat inside in a temporary place, waiting to be laid to rest.

For a long time, there was no evidence of the emotional toll that this was taking on my mother. She had been going along fine, holding herself together. But a simple incident caused her to unravel. She had arranged to meet a friend for coffee and was rushing to find her work uniform so she could go straight to the hospital afterwards to start her midday shift. She was running late and did not have the woman's telephone number to let her know. Gail arrived at the café about fifteen minutes after the appointed time. Her friend wasn't there. The café staff confirmed that she had left. Gail would later learn that the woman had left because she was unwell, but in this moment she felt awful and thought her friend must have been annoyed.

Mum walked back to the car and slumped into the driver's seat. A wave of defeat washed over her. She felt completely beaten. She reached for her phone and called Carmel, who she knew would have something comforting to say. Before she could speak, Gail began to weep. She couldn't stop, and as she tried to explain she was sobbing. Carmel knew a broken coffee date wasn't the cause for Gail's tears. This simple thing had triggered something much bigger, and Carmel put it into words: 'Gail, you have got so much going on. You're juggling work, Lifehouse, all these talks you give. You're worried about Juliette and James. You're wondering if you should sell the house. You're concerned about money. There's so much sadness for Chris and our darling Addy. You've got all those practical things to deal with. And there are the ashes.'

Especially the fate of the ashes. Carmel had vocalised what Gail felt. Gail knew her husband and son needed to be together and in the earth. Not having settled that created immense internal strain that she carried every day. She realised that finding a place for their ashes was the most important thing right now.

She had been told of the Northern Suburbs Memorial Gardens in Sydney's north, where there were beautiful places that could be bought. Gail had a look online and saw a small landscaped area with a garden seat that looked out over the Lane Cove National Park. She made an appointment immediately.

As she sat in a light and airy reception area waiting to be taken into the office, a man stepped through a doorway. 'I'm Stuart!' he said. 'I used to play guitar with Chris.' It turned out that Stuart lived next door to us once and, being a great guitar player, he had regularly come over to jam with Chris and his guitar teacher, Peter Pik. Stuart knew everything that had happened. He was gentle and kind to Gail. It was another of those coincidences.

Stuart drove Gail around the stunning gardens, with their open avenues and private circles, the towering green trees that hung over flowers and bush rock. They arrived at a row of plots near a large rose garden. White pebbles were scattered over small curved areas, framed by evergreen hedges. Each memorial had a plaque at its head and wooden seat at the foot. They were on the edge of the gardens, under the shade of large silky oaks and overlooking the wild ruggedness of the national park. It was serene, peaceful and private. Here, the ashes could be with the earth, rather than confined in a capsule. Gail noticed that a boy who had been Adam's age when he died was just two stations up. It felt right. They went back to the office to discuss the details.

'They're not cheap,' Stuart warned her. Gail expected that, although the amount he quoted far exceeded anything she had guessed. It was hugely expensive. But Gail had already made up her mind. She had been paralysed for so long. Now she was unstoppable. She resolved to dip into her superannuation.

A short time later she received a phone call from her financial adviser at Westpac, asking her to give a talk at BT Financial's meeting of advisers. The subject of the talk was holistic treatment of people and how lessons might be applied to looking after a person's financial wellbeing as well as their physical health. The best thing about the job was that it paid. Gail's talk was so successful that BT asked her to travel around Australia, speaking in every capital city about financial wellbeing after a serious diagnosis. Gail laughed about being the 'talent' on a road show. Then she learned that the fee was the exact amount that the memorial garden plot would cost. 'Westpac has given me so much more than money,' Gail told her adviser. 'You have unburdened me of this huge thing to deal with: my husband's and my son's ashes.'

When we did eventually place the ashes of my father and brother in the ground, it was with a feeling of rest. Wrapped in earth, under dappled light by the bush, they are together now. At home, without their ashes any more, my mother could finally rest also. The physical remains of her husband and son had gone, but their spirits had not.

Pocket Rocket

The seven-year anniversary of Dad's first cranial operation was on 30 November 2013. Again, we were at RPA, metres away from the jacaranda tree where Mum and I had sat together while he was on the operating table down below. But this day was not one of despair; it was a day of joy. Chris O'Brien Lifehouse had opened its doors to patients, and we were at a party to celebrate. The centre was to open progressively and this first stage saw all aspects of cancer care rolled out for outpatients including chemotherapy, radiation therapy and day surgery. Education, research and complementary therapies would begin, as well as clinical trials, allied health and emotional support. Specialist clinics for a number of cancer types were opening, including breast surgery, gynaecological oncology, head and neck, radiation and medical oncology and chemotherapy.

A few weeks earlier the freshly minted prime minister of Australia had visited — Tony Abbott, whose party had won the general election in September. Mr Abbott was the fifth successive prime minister to take office since Chris had begun lobbying for a centre of excellence seven years before. Over that time, the travelling circus of politicians and staffers had intermittently entered the Chris O'Brien Lifehouse orbit. Kevin Rudd had been a loyal supporter through both his terms as prime minister, as was Labor MP Tanya Plibersek, in whose seat Chris O'Brien Lifehouse sat. She always hugged my mother warmly when they met. Tony Abbott stood in the vast light-filled atrium. 'I never expected to find myself standing here, in this capacity,' he said with a smile.

On the evening of 30 November, hundreds of people who had worked to create this place came together. The room was filled with energy and excitement: everybody could take deep satisfaction in the result of what 'a critical mass of people with a unity of purpose', as Chris said, had achieved. Journalist Helen Dalley, an elegant MC, told the room that she had filled the same role for Chris and Gail back in 2002 at the launch of the Sydney Head and Neck Cancer Institute. She spoke about that first ball and how much had happened since in the past eleven and a half years.

My mother was the last speaker. I stood at the back as I listened to her speech for the first time — she no longer asked that I be the ears for her to practise upon. 'Today has been a most significant and wondrous day,' she said. Her voice was strong and measured. 'On this day, seven years ago, I sat in the perioperative room at RPAH with my much-adored husband, Chris O'Brien, and my daughter, before he was taken away from us to have his beautiful brain opened surgically in an attempt to remove a cancer that was threatening his life. The devastating news of this diagnosis had only been delivered to us days earlier and he had spent the previous few days on high-dose steroids. I can still see him, magnificent in the calm acceptance of his fate.

'A piece of paper that was pinned to a notice board caught my eye,' she continued. 'The admitting sister photocopied it for me and I still have it. It says: *YOU MUST NOT QUIT*. It went on to say that things don't always work out the way we plan them … and in the midst of the confusion, we wonder how things could ever be right again. But things have a way of working out and sometimes they work out better than we ever dreamed they could. This may be one of those times. Prophetic.

'Chris said publicly on many occasions that no Australian should ever have to go to the United States for their cancer treatment and that we should not be relying on the US to come up with all the breakthroughs. Chris started the narrative. He took control of the narrative and his opinion piece in the *Sydney Morning Herald* after his diagnosis fused the notion of comprehensive cancer centres with his illness. However, the learning to us, through his illness, was that cancer care, and indeed the care of any patient, needs to be holistic. A holistic approach, looking after a person's body, mind and spirit, has been a crusade for me for the last four years. This is a direct result of the fact that, on three separate occasions, Chris's illness, the death of our son two years ago and another child's serious illness last year … despite my medical connections, I found the system anything but patient-centred and holistic. However, I now feel fortunate that armed with an experiential understanding and a place to stand, I have been able to play my own role in making a meaningful contribution towards change. And now — finally — after seven years, the wheels of Chris O'Brien Lifehouse are officially in motion.

'Although it may seem like the end of a long journey, we are all aware that this is really just the beginning of a new chapter for Chris O'Brien Lifehouse, to now — in Chris's own words — "burn on discovery, to live for discovery" … with a unity of purpose aimed at innovation and improving patient outcomes. I value the extraordinary diversity of relationships I have been privileged to develop over the past four years. There are many people here tonight — and some not able to make it — who have all put their absolute heart and soul into this project. And despite our variety of beliefs and desires I know we have all been powerfully significant to each other's personal development as well as to this very honourable cause. I thank each and every one of you for what you have contributed. It has been a true coming together of the human spirit — and this is exactly what Chris brought out in people.

'The Chris O'Brien name will always continue to inspire hope, trust and integrity. To those who are entrusted with the name for the time you are here at Chris O'Brien Lifehouse, I wish you well as you enter a new chapter of creating the ethos and producing the results that will put us on the world stage as the gold standard of integrated, holistic, patient-centred cancer care.

'As Chris, the renaissance man, said at the end of his speech at the launch of Lifehouse in 2009, "it is a consummation devoutly to be wished".'

Jenny — my mother's dear friend who had convinced her to apply for residency at RPA all those years before — looked at me and said, 'That was her best yet, don't you think?' I agreed.

My mother stepped down from the podium and sank into the crowd. I found her with Jan and Max Moore Wilton, Jan with both her hands on Gail's cheeks, squeezing them as if she was one of her grandchildren. 'I'm just so proud of you,' she said. Then, she looked down at Gail's petite frame. 'But you're just so little, there's nothing of you!'

'She's a pocket rocket,' Max boomed. He wrapped his arms around her in the same way that Adam would have.

At a function a few weeks later, I was seated next to Peter Overton at dinner — the gentlemanly Channel 9 reporter who had entered our lives seven years previously when Dad was first diagnosed. He had done several reports since then and stayed in close contact with the family over the years, emceeing many Chris O'Brien Lifehouse functions. 'You know,' Peter said, 'it has been such a privilege watching your family throughout this period, especially your mother. We've seen a transformation in her.'

'Do you think so?' I asked. We both looked at my mother, seated across the table. She was chatting with those on either side of her. She laughed, throwing her head back and revealing that splendid smile.

'Yes,' he said. 'She has absolutely transformed.'

At the time I genuinely agreed. But now, after many hours of contemplation while writing this book, it has occurred to me that perhaps my mother has not been transformed. Perhaps Gail has been revealed.

Dear Mum,

Recently, I had the flu and was coughing through the night. I couldn't sleep, so got out of bed in the wee hours to make tea. You appeared, tapped on James's door and asked if he knew where the cough medicine was. I sat on a stool and watched as you and Jamie, in your dressing gowns and with blurry eyes, opened every cupboard and drawer looking for the medicine for me. It made my heart ache. Watching you both, I realised how much I still have. How rich we are still.

As I write this, I am sitting in the library at the University of Sydney, looking across the green lawn to the university's Great Hall. That majestic stone building has stood witness to many milestones in your story: your and Dad's graduations, marriage, Dad's doctorate of surgery at the zenith of his career, an oration on his transition from esteemed doctor to terminal patient. A year after he died, his face shone through the hall in a large projected image at a memorial fundraiser. The image hung over you, Mum. While you stood in his place at the lectern.

So much has happened but a stone's throw from that Great Hall. It would seem we haven't come very far. But we have travelled galaxies in our hearts and minds. What an odyssey it is, just to be and to love in this life.

With a heart full of love, Juliette

* * *

My darling Juliette,

With deepest gratitude I write you this final letter. You have pieced together the jigsaw of this tale with such grace and skill. As you are aware, I had been approached by publishers on several occasions over the last few years to write about caring for your father. I not only found the task too daunting but the story seemed to keep unfolding. It did not end with his death. Instead, another door opened.

You ask me whether I ever thought I would be capable of doing all that I have done these last few years. The answer is simple: I never thought about it, it just happened. (But if I had given it any thought at all, the answer would have been, most certainly not.)

As your father wrote in his memoir, 'life is not a linear experience but rather a circular process, as if it all began when myriad pebbles were cast upon a vast pool'.

It's important to just keep putting one foot in front of the other. Each day, the sun also rises. In the words of Thích Nhất Hạnh, a Vietnamese Buddhist monk and teacher, 'Breathing in I calm my body, breathing out I smile, twenty-four brand new hours lie before me.'

I have learned the hard way to go with the flow and try not to resist or force. Perhaps there is indeed a map for each and every one of us to follow if only we will listen and trust. Certainly opportunities present themselves and we have the choice to either take action or not. We have free will.

Regarding Chris O'Brien Lifehouse, I think of it as a place of healing, rather than cure. There is so much more to cancer than simply killing malignant cells.

For myself, I am not afraid of that final sleep. I know there is nothing to fear. Surely Hamlet was pointing out how little even the most educated people can explain when he said, 'There are more things in heaven and earth, Horatio, than are dreamt of in your philosophy.'

We have in our small household a spectrum of personalities, attitudes and beliefs. But your father and brother are ever-present in each of us, my darling. It is as the poet Robert Fitzgerald wrote and is inscribed on the plaque that rests over your father's ashes beside those of our beloved son: 'Time is a fool if it thinks to have ended, one single splendid thing that has been.'

With my love, Mum

Acknowledgments

Dear reader,

I deeply appreciate being given the opportunity to share my mother's and family's story, and am grateful to you for having read it. I do not believe in the slightest that our story is unique. Rather, I'd hoped that it would be worth sharing for the opposite reason: its themes and our experiences are as universal as they are remarkable.

The origins of this book lie in the days when my mother and father were promoting his memoir, *Never Say Die*. Quite unexpectedly we discovered an interest in my mother's, the carer's, account. As her story kept unfolding, I encouraged her to write the book which I believed beckoned. Later, it occurred to me that perhaps I could write it instead.

In my attempt to distil our busy and unscripted lives into a coherent narrative, I was faced with countless difficult decisions about what to include. Innumerable moments and friends have been omitted from these pages, but that is no reflection of how important they have been to us. I did my best to be guided by what I thought the reader might need and like to know.

This particularly applies to the passages about Chris O'Brien Lifehouse, which I must emphasise exists today because of hundreds of hard-working people who have played their own integral roles and been passionate to see it succeed. I did not intend for this book to lay claim to any glory, nor did I wish to diminish the achievements and contributions of others. I selected moments which shed light on my mother's story and the themes therein. Today, more than ever, Chris O'Brien Lifehouse is driven by visionary and compassionate professionals. It truly is a critical mass of people with a unity of purpose.

I would also like to acknowledge the source of a reflection on page 88. The idea of hope resting between the x-axis on a graph and the curve that is falling towards it came from an enlightening conversation I had with Dr Charlie Teo.

Over the last two years, my mum has played a huge role in pulling this work together. She has spent countless hours being interviewed and dictating her answers, pored through old files and spoken to friends in order to reconstruct events, laboured over her letters and checked my work. I am forever indebted to her.

I am also thankful to Paul Cave, Bill Conley, Bob Rose, and Samuel Taufa (aka Junior) for their help reconstructing events, and Karen Bristow and Dominique Galea for their feedback on certain sections.

I was lucky to benefit from the expertise and advice of two dear friends and writers, who generously read my entire work: Stephanie Dowrick, who has been my teacher and mentor through this process and empowered me throughout, and Tom Ross, whose talent and friendship inspire and spur me on.

I have also found immense support and camaraderie in the friendships I've made in two groups: from a young writers' group, the creative influences of Tom Ross, Augusto Mallman and Thomas De Angelis have enriched my writing. And from a course titled Writers Workshop with Stephanie Dowrick at the Faber Writing Academy at Allen & Unwin, Helen Greenacre, Jenny Levy, Father Peter McGrath, Sarah Menary, Katy Morgan, Sheridan Rogers, Penelope Smith and Fiona Hargraves have been wonderful companions on this journey.

My deep gratitude goes to the staff at HarperCollins Publishers for taking this project on (and sticking with it!). Catherine Milne and Amruta Slee were patient guides and Rachel Dennis, Pam Dunne and Jacqueline Kent improved the book considerably through the editing process. Matt Stanton's creative talents produced a lovely cover and he was very gracious in his approach.

Finally, if it weren't for Stephanie Raethel, my editor at Fairfax and Bauer Media, this book would probably not have happened. It was no more than an idea when I embellished its progress during a job interview with Stephanie, but her encouragement that I should find a publisher prompted me to commit to the work. It's lucky I was so naive about how difficult it would be or else I probably would never have undertaken it.

About the Author

Juliette Isabella O'Brien was born in Sydney, Australia, in 1984. After graduating from high school she studied a Bachelor of Arts in Communications (majoring in journalism) at the University of Technology, Sydney, and later a Bachelor of Laws at the University of Sydney. She is admitted as a solicitor in NSW but does not practise law. She works in digital media and is currently employed at SBS. This is her first book.